THE NATURAL WORLD OF
LEWIS AND CLARK

THE NATURAL WORLD OF
LEWIS AND CLARK

❧

David A. Dalton

UNIVERSITY OF MISSOURI PRESS

COLUMBIA AND LONDON

Copyright © 2008 by
The Curators of the University of Missouri
University of Missouri Press, Columbia, Missouri 65201
Printed and bound in China
All rights reserved
5 4 3 2 1   11 10 09 08 07

Library of Congress Cataloging-in-Publication Data

Dalton, David A.
  The natural world of Lewis and Clark / David A. Dalton.
    p. cm.
  Summary: "Dalton reexamines many of Lewis and Clark's discoveries,
and their identification of new plants and animals, in the light of modern
science to show their lasting biological significance. In clear, readily
accessible terms, he relates the Expedition's observations to principles
of ecology, genetics, physiology, and animal behavior"--Provided by
publisher.
  Includes bibliographical references and index.
  ISBN 978-0-8262-1766-0 (alk. paper)
 1. Natural history--West (U.S.) 2. Lewis and Clark Expedition
(1804-1806) I. Title.
  QH104.5.W4D35 2007
  508.78--dc22

                                                    2007024967

Designer and Compositor: Kristie Lee
Printer and Binder: Everbest Printing company through
    Four Colour Imports, Louisville, KY
Typeface: Adobe Caslon

*For Ingrid and Barbara, without whose help
this book would not have been possible*

CONTENTS

ILLUSTRATIONS

Figures

Tables

PREFACE

⸙

T he journey of Lewis and Clark is a defining moment in American history that has attracted the attention and imagination of inquisitive minds since the last ripples faded away on the muddy Missouri in 1806. The national interest intensified even more with the arrival of the bicentennial celebration. Authors have published hundreds of books, most notably Gary Moulton's comprehensive and defining thirteen-volume series, *The Journals of the Lewis and Clark Expedition* (University of Nebraska Press, 1983–2001), from which all the quotations in this book derive. Several excellent television documentaries have aired on PBS, the History Channel, and elsewhere. The World Wide Web contains a vast amount of information of the highest quality on sites maintained by the Smithsonian Institution, National Geographic Society, Academy of Natural Sciences, Missouri Historical Society, and others. Perhaps the most complete Web site is Discovering Lewis and Clark, http://www.lewis-clark.org.

Part of the attraction lies in the fact that the "Expedition" (no further descriptor is necessary, unless it would be to emphasize *THE*) means so many different things to different people. To the historian, it is the complex story of how human activities and personalities determined the fate of a great nation. To the humanist, it is the story of perhaps the most universal mind of the time, Jefferson, and how his intellect forged such all-encompassing visions. To the anthropologist, it is an invaluable early account of Native peoples. To the linguist, it is a fascinating study in the art of travel journals and in creative spelling. To the literary scholar and classicist, it is the American version of Homer's *Odyssey* complete with savage beasts and superhuman challenges. To the adventurer, it is the account of the mission missed by accident of being born some two hundred years too late. To the natural historian, it is a chance to share in the excitement of the discovery of the natural wonders of the West, often at the time of their initial description by Euro-Americans. The story works on so many levels that it is nearly inexhaustible.

This book is my attempt, as a professional biologist, to reexamine some of the scientific discoveries of the Expedition in the light of modern science. Much has already been written about how Lewis and Clark discovered so much that was new to science, in particular the hundreds of previously unknown plant and animal species. It is not my intention to catalog these findings, since this has already been done so excellently elsewhere. The reader is referred to Paul Cutright's outstanding book *Lewis and Clark: Pioneering Naturalists* (2d ed., 2003), which is the standard-bearer for its thoroughness and approachable narrative style. A more encyclopedic coverage of the flora, along with excellent color photographs, can be found in *Lewis and Clark's Green World: The Expedition and Its Plants* by A. Scott Earle and James L. Reveal (2003).

My intention is to look at the story behind the story. There is almost always a deeper issue to probe—another rock, slightly more distant perhaps, to look under. What were the lasting scientific impacts of the Expedition's discoveries? What is it about the ecology, taxonomy, physiology, and other -ologies of these plants and animals that continues to draw the interest of scientists today? Once I started down this road, the problem was not in finding enough material, but rather in finding where to stop without getting too bogged down in technical detail. Much of what is exciting in modern biology these days involves work with DNA, proteins, and computers. Does this relate to stories from Lewis and Clark? Absolutely—in hundreds of ways. If we are going to explore these issues in some detail, we are going to have to at least touch on some technical issues such as the PCR (polymerase chain reaction) technique or others with intimidating names. Would you like to know what extinct giant ground sloths ate? You need PCR. Would you like to know why Indians were right to use cottonwood bark as winter feed for horses? You will need a few special techniques. Why is it that some particularly nasty invasive weeds have so thoroughly changed much of the western landscape since Lewis and Clark passed through? If you really want to know, you will need to use some up-to-date tools. Throughout this book I have not shied away from introducing these tools and techniques when needed. I have tried to do so gently, keeping as my target readers who are intelligent and curious but not trained as specialists in science. When appropriate, I have included a nontechnical primer that will allow you to get past the names and straight to the meat of the matter.

Speaking of names, the reader will find quite a few Latin names for plants and animals in this book. I have included the common names as well, but I encourage you to view the more technical names with an open mind. Lewis certainly did, and he had only a few weeks of technical training in the Linnaean system. Besides, much of the lore of these organisms has to do with the Latin names. So don't be afraid to jump in. And especially don't worry about the proper pronunciations. All the native Latin speakers have been gone a long time, and nobody really knows how any of it should be pronounced anyway.

Many readers may be surprised to learn that a considerable number of the original plant specimens collected by Lewis and Clark still exist, mostly under the protection of the Academy of Natural Sciences in Philadelphia. High-quality images of the entire collection are available on the Web for the academy as well as in published form.[1] These images as well as much relevant background information are available on a CD that can be purchased from the academy for about twenty dollars. There are 239 of these specimens, and their historical and scientific value is tremendous.[2] Many of these specimens are "types," meaning that they are the actual specimens that the botanist Frederick Pursh used to describe the species. As such, these specimens are the ultimate reference for modern botanists who might need to establish the identity or characteristics of a particular plant with absolute certainty. Does this mean that botanists must jet off to Philadelphia whenever they need to identify Lewis's bitterroot (*Lewisia rediviva*)? Of course not. In fact, the collection is seldom, if ever, consulted for such a mundane purpose. The greatest value of the collection is a historical one. Perhaps it is useful to make an analogy to the U.S. Constitution. Senators, judges, lawyers, and other legal types are (we hope) diligent in adhering to the strictures of the Constitution, but they do not feel the need to consult the original document at the National Archives on a regular basis. Yet obviously that document is of incalculable value. In the same way, the Lewis and Clark plant collection is a national treasure. Each specimen has its own story, both with respect to the events surrounding its discovery and gathering and with respect to what it can tell us about what is going on out there in the nature of the American West today.

1. See Moulton, *Journals of the Expedition,* vol. 12.
2. Ibid., 7.

THE NATURAL WORLD OF
LEWIS AND CLARK

CHAPTER 1

⌘

Mega-expectations

I t is hard to appreciate fully just how little early Americans knew about the country west of the Mississippi. Thomas Jefferson was arguably the greatest intellectual on the continent, yet even he had almost no idea what was out there. It is instructive to examine some particular points where Jefferson went astray.

Jefferson believed that the West probably still contained many of the great mammals of the Pleistocene epoch, including mammoths, giant ground sloths, and perhaps others. He believed this because many mammoth bones had been found in the East—especially in Kentucky at a place called Big Bone Lick. Meriwether Lewis visited Big Bone Lick as he passed through Cincinnati on his way to St. Louis on September 28, 1803, at which time he collected some mammoth fossils and shipped them to Jefferson.

Jefferson was an avid collector of fossils, many of which he displayed at Monticello. He also came into possession of some fossil bones of a giant ground sloth from present-day West Virginia and

1

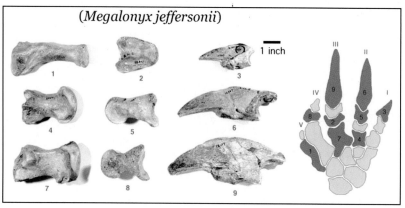

Fig. 1.1. Modern photograph of the hand bones of the *Megalonyx* that were described by Jefferson. Courtesy of Academy of Natural Sciences.

subsequently wrote one of the first technical papers in North America in the field of paleontology in 1799 (fig. 1.1).[1] He called the beast a "Great-Claw," or *Megalonyx*, which he estimated to be at least three times larger than an African lion. Jefferson went into considerable detail to describe the dimensions of these bones. For instance, the "Great-Claw" itself was 7.5 inches long (as opposed to 1.4 inches for a lion's claw), and the diameter at the middle of the femur was 4.25 inches, whereas the lion comes in at only 1.15 inches. Jefferson speculated that such a creature could easily dine on mammoths in the way that he imagined that modern African lions might prey on elephants. Not only was Jefferson one of the first paleontologists, but he was also an ecologist, as evidenced by his concern about the fate of *Megalonyx*. He noted:

1. Jefferson, "A Memoir of the Discovery of Certain Bones of a Quadruped of the Clawed Type in the Western Parts of Virginia." Despite its antiquity, this article is readily available online at many libraries. It makes for some entertaining reading.

In fine, the bones exist: therefore the animal has existed. The movements of nature are in a never ending circle. The animal species which has once been put into a train of motion, is still probably moving in that train. For if one link in nature's chain might be lost, another and another might be lost, till this whole system of things should vanish by piece-meal. . . . If this animal then has once existed, it is probable on this general view of the movements of nature that he still exists.

Jefferson later instructed Lewis to be on the lookout for such unusual creatures but did not mention them by name. Instead, the charge was to look for "the animals of the country generally, & especially those not known in the U.S. the remains and accounts of any which may [be] deemed rare or extinct."[2] But Lewis and Clark were about twelve thousand years too late, for reasons we will examine shortly.

Jefferson also had peculiar ideas of what the western Indians might be like. He was familiar with a popular legend of the time that held that a band of Welshmen with Viking roots settled in North America in the twelfth century. There are many fragments of stories from early Europeans—mostly secondhand hearsay—that described encounters with white Indians who spoke Welsh. In particular, the Mandan, who were unusually fair-skinned and with whom Lewis and Clark spent their winter in North Dakota, were often mentioned as likely candidates for this distinction. If this sounds too bizarre to be true, that's because it is just that—too bizarre. Lewis and Clark found no evidence for it. However, the legend is still with us today and has a few fringe advocates even in academe. It is a myth that just won't die, though the evidence is woefully thin.

2. Reuben G. Thwaites, *Original Journals of the Lewis and Clark Expedition,* 7:249.

Jefferson also held out the possibility that Lewis and Clark might encounter a long-lost tribe of Israelites in the guise of American Indians. This belief persists today as part of the teachings of the Mormon Church. Recent DNA evidence has debunked this bizarre theory, but there are still a few believers.[3] So, no Welshmen and no Israelites—unless you want to include Lewis, who was in fact of Welsh descent.

Jefferson also assumed that the climate west of the Mississippi was similar to that in Kentucky and Virginia, that is, temperate with ample rainfall and thus suitable to agriculture. This was a myth that was long in dying, dragging out after the Civil War in the misguided belief that "rain follows the plow" and perhaps even contributing to hardships of the Dust Bowl on the Great Plains in the 1930s.

Before the Expedition, no one understood the major geographical features of the West. Jefferson believed that all the great rivers of the West—including the Columbia, Colorado, Rio Grande, and Missouri—arose from a single "height of land" and that it might be possible to completely traverse the continent with only a brief portage across the mountains. He believed this in part because he was aware that Alexander Mackenzie, a fur trader with the North West Company, succeeded in crossing virtually all of Canada by river in 1793. He went up the Peace River from the east and made a brief portage of only seven hundred yards, at which point he was able to eventually connect to the Fraser River, which drains into the Pacific. The elevation at the portage was only three thousand feet.[4] This remarkable feat is less famous than the later Lewis and Clark Expedition in part because Mackenzie had no interest in science or

---

3. See Simon G. Southerton, *Losing a Lost Tribe: Native Americans, DNA, and the Mormon Church.*

4. Stephen Ambrose, *Undaunted Courage: Meriwether Lewis, Thomas Jefferson, and the Opening of the American West,* 73.

ethnology and so had less impact. His interest was strictly commercial, and in this sense he was phenomenally successful, eventually becoming one of the wealthiest men in England (and a knight). But he rarely wrote of the plants and animals he encountered, and when he did it was with very little insight. For instance, he referred to mountain goats as "small white buffalo" and freely admitted,

> I do not possess the science of the naturalist; and even if the qualifications of that character had been attained by me, its curious spirit would not have been gratified. I could not stop to dig into the earth, over whose surface I was compelled to pass with rapid steps; nor could I turn aside to collect plants which nature might have scattered on the way, when my thoughts were anxiously employed in making provision for the day that was passing over me.[5]

Nevertheless, Mackenzie's explorations were key in establishing a British presence and claim to ownership in western Canada. In this regard, Mackenzie played a similar role to that of Lewis and Clark's advancement of American interests to the south. Even though Mackenzie's adventure took place in 1793, it was not until 1801 that a book on the subject, *Voyages from Montreal,* was published. Jefferson got his hands on one of the first copies, which set him into a frenzy of activity to get his own expedition off the ground.

It was quite reasonable to assume—as apparently Jefferson did—that the Appalachians in Virginia were perhaps the highest mountains on the continent. The highest point in Virginia is Mount Rogers at 5,729 feet. Even though some high mountains such as Mount Hood (11,235 feet) in Oregon and Mount Rainier (14,410 feet) in Washington had been sighted and named thirteen years earlier on

---

5. Mackenzie, *Journal of the Voyage to the Pacific,* 49.

Captain George Vancouver's remarkable expedition to the western coast, the scale of these mountains was not widely appreciated until later. Lewis and Clark saw these and other high mountains of the Cascade Range, but they almost invariably misidentified them. For instance, they were actually looking at Mount St. Helens (not Mount Rainier) when on November 4, 1805, Ordway, a sergeant who also kept a dairy during the Expedition, wrote that they "discovred a high round mountain Some distance back from the River on the Stard Side which is called mount rainy." The highest point that Lewis and Clark actually set foot on was probably Saddle Mountain (8,225 feet) as they entered the Bitterroot Valley during their tortuous crossing of the Rocky Mountains.

It is clear that Jefferson had some pretty strange ideas in spite of the fact that he was certainly a genius and had the largest library in the world on the subject of the geography of North America. The fact is, nobody really knew what to expect. If such an expedition were to be launched today, Jefferson might tell Lewis to be on the lookout for Bigfoot, space aliens, and weapons of mass destruction. They could be there, and as any good scientist can tell you, "absence of evidence is not evidence of absence."

There are numerous interesting biological issues surrounding the question of the missing mammoths and other large mammals—henceforth referred to as the megafauna that are defined as animals weighing more than one hundred pounds. The big mammals had not been gone long—only something like twelve thousand years, which puts them squarely at the end of the Pleistocene epoch. The bones of the megafauna that have been found are not fossilized in the sense that dinosaur bones are. The bones have simply been preserved more or less intact, usually in caves or buried in mud or permafrost. There are even cases of mummified remains of complete skeletons, flesh, skin, hair, and dung.

The diversity and size of the megafauna are absolutely astounding. Jefferson's *Megalonyx* was an impressive beast that probably weighed in around eight hundred pounds, but that animal had plenty of large cousins, including about thirty-four genera of other ground sloths in the Americas. The biggest was *Megatherium* (literally, "great beast"), which may have topped eight thousand pounds—a bulk that puts it in the range of a modern African elephant.

Ground sloths, mastodons, and mammoths are only the beginning of a very strange assortment of beasts. Beavers back then were approximately the size of bears (four to five hundred pounds). Lewis and Clark often spotted California condors along the Columbia River, but they missed out on their giant ancestors—the teratorns, which were giant vultures with wingspans of up to sixteen feet in North America and perhaps twenty-five feet in South America (fig. 1.2). Nevertheless, the condor is an impressive bird, as Clark noted on February 16, 1806: "I believe this to be the largest Bird of North America.[6] it was not in good order and yet it wayed 25 lbs had it have been so it might very well have weighed 10 lbs. more or 35 lbs. between the extremities of the wings it measured 9 feet 2 Inches." That is a big bird, but still far short of the teratorns.[7] The glyptodont—a type of giant armadillo—weighed in around three thousand pounds and had an armored shell two inches thick. Other examples include fossil rhinos, horses, and camels such as those found in ash beds in Nebraska in which the bones are still articulated and joined together

6. He was correct.

7. A recent study has suggested that the reason the condor persisted into modern times is that its food base included large marine mammals that survived the Pleistocene extinctions. In contrast, the teratorns were restricted to the land animals that of course largely disappeared. See Kena Fox-Dobbs et al., "Dietary Controls on Extinction versus Survival among Avian Megafauna in the Late Pleistocene."

Fig. 1.2. Typical examples of the North American megafauna of the Late Pleistocene. *Left to right:* teratorn vulture (flying, *Teratornis*), mammoth (*Mammuthus*), musk ox (background, *Ovibos*), ancient bison (*Bison*), saber-toothed cat (*Smilodon*), dire wolf (*Canis*), horse (background, *Equus*), giant ground sloth (*Megatherium*), giant armadillo (*Glyptodon*), and camel (background, *Camelops*). Copyright 2000 Yale Peabody Museum and Rudolph Zallinger.

in the proper order. Some specimens contained unborn young and stomach contents, thus giving paleontologists an opportunity to reconstruct the life appearance and habits of these ancient species with great accuracy.

North America lost thirty-three of its forty-seven genera of megafauna in the Late Pleistocene. Meanwhile, South America lost fifty of its fifty-nine genera of megafauna. In many regards, the changes that took place in the few thousand years before Lewis and Clark were more severe than the changes that have taken place since. It must have been quite a sight to see the North American plains filled with camels, ground sloths, and mammoths instead of cows and wheat fields.

Since organic remains, and not just mineralized fossils, of these mammals have been found, it has been possible to apply techniques in modern molecular biology to great effect. For instance, the sequence of mammoth mitochondrial DNA is now known in its entirety. It may even be possible to obtain something approaching a complete nuclear genomic sequence for mammoths, thus raising the possibility of a new field called "paleogenomics."[8] This would be invaluable for studying population genetics of Pleistocene mammals and plants and might even shed light on causes of their extinction. However, reconstructing a complete, living mammoth using DNA sequence is not practical, and thus a "Pleistocene Park" scenario with living mammoths is unlikely.

The power of ancient DNA studies was demonstrated recently by scientists who reconstructed the diet of giant sloths from Nevada by analyzing the DNA in vegetable remnants in their dung. This group used the PCR technique to sequence a short section of the rubisco gene (*rbcL*)—a key gene in all plants that allows them to photosynthesize. They could then match up the DNA sequence with known sequences in extant plants to determine what the sloths were eating (table 1.1). The older ones (28,500 years ago) were eating mostly pine, mulberry, and capers, whereas their descendants from 11,000 years ago ate mostly mints, sunflowers, and saltbush. It is clear that these animals were herbivores with a wide-ranging palette and not carnivores, as Jefferson once thought. The "Great-Claw" threw him off.

8. See H. N. Poinar et al., "Metagenomics to Paleogenomics: Large-Scale Sequencing of Mammoth DNA."

Table 1.1. Plant species eaten by giant ground sloths from Nebraska 11,000 to 28,500 years ago

Family	Number of genera	Representative genera
Sunflower	9	*Achillea, Lactuca*
Mustard	8	*Brassica*
Rose	7	not given
Mint	4	not given
Grass	3	*Stipa, Karroochloa*
Caper	2	not given
Saltbush	2	*Atriplex, Grayia*
Willow	2	*Salix, Populus*
Agave	1	*Yucca*
Nolina	1	*Nolina*
Grape	1	*Vitis*
Mulberry	1	*Morus*
Pine	1	*Pinus*
Creosote bush	1	*Larrea*
Milkweed	1	not given

Source: M. Hofreiter et al., "A Molecular Analysis of Ground Sloth Diet through the Last Glaciation."

Note: The identification is based on DNA sequences from chloroplast DNA isolated from dung.

So what happened to all these animals? The short answer is humans ate them. Climate change may have also been a factor, but there is good evidence that we—or, more precisely, those early humans who walked across the land bridge over the Bering Strait about thirteen thousand years ago—did it. The case for this theory was put forth

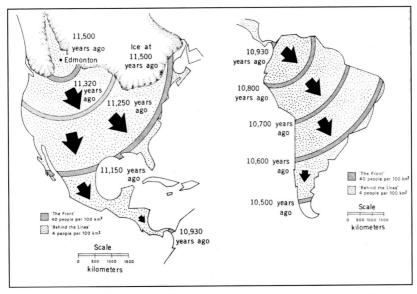

Fig. 1.3. The wavelike sweep of human migration into the Americas. From Paul S. Martin, "The Discovery of America," 972. Reprinted with permission. Copyright 1973 American Association for the Advancement of Science.

in 1973 by Paul Martin, a geology professor at the University of Arizona (fig. 1.3).[9] Since that time, the story has been clouded a bit by evidence suggesting a limited human presence somewhat earlier and perhaps a role for climate change. The issue is far from settled. There are many adamant voices that argue either for or against the role of humans in the extinctions, but the case that Martin made is still largely intact with considerable fossil and paleoanthropological evidence to back it up.

According to the "overkill" hypothesis that Martin put forth, early humans found a huge surplus of naive, inexperienced animals that

9. See Paul S. Martin, "The Discovery of America."

had never seen humans and were thus easy prey. Why should a three thousand–pound ground sloth be concerned by the proximity of a feeble one hundred–pound human? Martin called them "ambulatory pin cushions" and even went so far as to suggest that adolescent humans might have amused themselves by using them just for target practice.[10] The humans wiped out the megafauna before there was time for the animals to learn or evolve appropriate defenses. The hunters rode their success in a line of death first through North America and then South America, wiping out the local populations of large animals as they marched south in search of continued abundance of game. The leading front of this wave could have supported a dense population of humans (one person per square mile) that migrated at perhaps about ten miles per year. Martin estimated that, from a starting population of only one hundred humans, it would have taken only about seventeen generations to saturate the hemisphere. Local extinctions would have occurred within a decade of the wave hitting any particular area.

Some of the more compelling evidence that humans were primarily responsible for the disappearance of the megafauna includes: (1) the paleological record that shows a correlation between the arrival of humans and extinction of the megafauna; (2) the fact that the megafauna had been around for tens of millions of years over various climate changes and then vanished nearly overnight—mere decades, if we believe Martin; and (3) the fact that the only large animals that did survive beyond human arrival are those that avoided humans either by being nocturnal, arboreal, alpine, or deep-forest dwellers. This last point argues especially compellingly against the climate-change theory. Last, recent sophisticated computer models based on human

---

10. See Paul S. Martin, *Twilight of the Mammoths: Ice Age Extinctions and the Rewilding of America*.

hunting and growth rates have correctly predicted the extinction or survival of thirty-two out of forty-one prey species without invoking climate-change effects.[11] Readers interested in exploring further the issue of extinction of the megafauna should refer to Martin's 2006 book, *Twilight of the Mammoths: Ice Age Extinctions and the Rewilding of America.* Regardless of the cause—hunting ("overkill"), climate change ("overchill"), or disease ("overill")—the fact remains undisputed that the megafauna did go extinct around this time, and thus the ecosystems of the American West changed radically only a few thousand years before Lewis and Clark's arrival.

Ecosystems left in the wake of these changes had much less diversity than the original ones. There are many studies in modern ecology demonstrating that the removal of just a few keystone species may result in the catastrophic collapse of species diversity.[12] Let's take just one case illustrating some likely ecological consequences of extinctions. Consider the case of the gomphotheres—a group of elephant-like creatures that roamed Central America and South America in the Pleistocene.[13] There are at least thirty-seven extant plant species that were probably highly dependent on the extinct megafauna, such as gomphotheres, for distribution of their fruit. The large and hard-skinned fruits were simply too tough for any smaller animal to crack open, much less carry off to a new site. Consequently, the abundance of these plants in modern neotropical forests and grasslands has been greatly reduced to the point that some plants appear to reproduce hardly at all, putting their future in doubt.

11. See John Alroy, "A Multispecies Overkill Simulation of the End-Pleistocene Megafaunal Mass Extinction."

12. See, for instance, R. T. Paine, "Intertidal Community Structure: Experimental Studies on the Relationship between a Dominant Competitor and Its Principal Predator."

13. See Daniel H. Janzen and Paul S. Martin, "Neotropical Anachronisms: The Fruits the Gomphotheres Ate."

Fig. 1.4. Lewis sitting in a garden in St. Louis preparing a letter to Jefferson in which he describes the samples of Osage orange that he was sending. Lewis's letter of March 26, 1804, begins: "Dear Sir: I send you herewith enclosed some slips of the great Osages Plums and Apples." From Jackson, *Letters of the Lewis and Clark Expedition*, 170. Artwork by Michael Haynes (http://www.mhaynesart.com/home.html).

Early in their journeys, Lewis and Clark ran across one such plant that appears to have lost its dispersers when the megafauna were wiped out. While still camped at Camp Dubois near St. Louis, Lewis observed Osage orange (*Maclura pomifera*) blooming and sent cuttings and seeds back to Jefferson (fig. 1.4). These may be the first objects returned to Jefferson by the Expedition.[14] Several impressive Osage orange trees still survive in Philadelphia that were started

14. Moulton, *Journals of the Expedition*, 2:210.

Fig. 1.5. Osage orange tree planted at St. Peter's Church (formerly the garden of Bernard McMahon; see Chapter 2) in Philadelphia. This tree, along with several similar ones in the background, is reputed to have been planted from seeds or cuttings sent back by Lewis. Photo by author.

from these same specimens (fig. 1.5). Offspring of the Philadelphia Osage orange trees eventually even made it to England, thanks to the efforts of David Douglas, the famous naturalist sent to North America by the Horticultural Society of London (later named the Royal Horticultural Society) to collect plants for English gardens. In 1823 Douglas visited Bernard McMahon's garden in Philadelphia, where he observed several Osage orange trees with a "height of about seventeen feet, bushy and rugged."[15] He obtained fruits from one of McMahon's fellow nurserymen, David Landreth, and carried

15. Douglas, *Journal Kept by David Douglas during His Travels in North America, 1823–1827*, 8.

them back to England for propagation. It is almost certain that this fruit came from plants that were descendants of cuttings sent back by Lewis.

Lewis wrote to Jefferson on March 26, 1804, that "so much do the savages esteem the wood of this tree for the purpose of making their bows, that they travel many hundreds miles in quest of it."[16] A local tribe of Indians known as the Spiroan Indians flourished in the area around A.D. 500–1300. This tribe was fortunate enough to control this restricted resource and consequently was very prosperous by local standards.[17]

Although Paul Cutright credits Lewis and Clark with introducing Osage orange to science, the tree had been encountered earlier by French explorers who named it *bois d'arc* ("bowwood").[18] This name may have been corrupted over time to the familiar "Ozark" to indicate the hills of Missouri and Arkansas where Osage orange grows, although there are alternative explanations for the origin of "Ozark."[19]

The fruits of Osage orange are so tough and large (two to three pounds) that hardly anything can eat them (fig. 1.6). In fact, Osage orange is probably the best example in North America of a fruit that now lacks its dispersers due to the disappearance of the megafauna.[20] By the time Europeans arrived, this species was clinging to a range restricted to a small area near where Arkansas, Texas, and Oklahoma meet. The actual range may have been so small as to be limited to

16. Donald Jackson, *Letters of the Lewis and Clark Expedition with Related Documents, 1783–1854*, 170.

17. Frank F. Schambach, "Osage Orange Bows, Indian Horses, and the Blackland Prairie of Northeastern Texas," 212.

18. Paul Cutright, *Lewis and Clark: Pioneering Naturalists*, 41.

19. See Richard Rhodes, *The Ozarks*.

20. Connie Barlow, *The Ghosts of Evolution: Nonsensical Fruit, Missing Partners, and Other Ecological Anachronisms*, 120.

Fig. 1.6. Fruit of the Osage orange (*Maclura pomifera*). Photo by Steven J. Baskauf (http://bioimages.Vanderbilt. edu).

just one watershed (the Bois d'Arc Creek). Yet fossil evidence indicates that this species ranged as far north as southern Ontario during the Pleistocene epoch. The thick pulp of the fruit repels rodents who might be tempted by the deeply embedded seeds. There are simply no extant animals who show any inclination to eat it.

Maclura is in the mulberry family (Moraceae) and has relatives from other parts of the world that are dispersed by extant megafauna. For example, *Treculia africana,* commonly known as African breadfruit, produces fruit with a diameter up to ten inches and is a favorite food of elephants. Similar examples can be found in other members of the Moraceae in Asia. The megafaunal traits of *Maclura* are so extreme that one wonders how it has managed to survive at all. Certainly, several other species of *Maclura* from North America did not survive the Pleistocene extinctions. Connie Barlow suggests that "root suckering, apomixis [nonsexual seed production] and the exceptional resistance to wood rot and termites are compensatory life history traits that could have held extinction at bay for thirteen thousand years."[21] Lewis and Clark were too late to help the ground sloths and mammoths, but they arrived just in time to start the process of pulling *Maclura* back from the brink of oblivion.

Why were the Pleistocene mammals so big? For that matter, why too the dinosaurs? There are several ways to answer that question. Generally speaking, the size of an animal increases with the landmass of the area they inhabit. A recent survey of the top terrestrial herbivores and carnivores over the past sixty-five thousand years confirmed this trend and also established a clear ranking of body sizes as follows: ectothermic (that is, cold-blooded) herbivore > endothermic (warm-blooded) herbivore > ectothermic carnivore > endothermic carnivore (fig. 1.7).

This ranking is due in part to the greater amount of food available to herbivores. A larger food base can support a larger body mass. Ectotherms are also favored for food caloric reasons, since they have a much lower energy requirement (per pound of body mass) than do endotherms. The logical extension of this argument is that an animal tends to be as big as its food base will allow. A larger landmass allows for larger home ranges of individuals, ergo more food and a larger animal. Other factors include a sort of ecological arms race in which herbivores tend to evolve larger body sizes in order to fend off would-be predators. Who would really want to tangle with an eight thousand–pound giant ground sloth or a twelve thousand–pound mammoth? Predators simply did not have the food base to get ahead in such a showdown. The ultimate mammalian expression of this battle was the case of the rhinoceros-like *Indricotherium* from Asia (alas, extinct for thirty million years) that stood sixteen feet high at the shoulders and weighed up to seventy thousand pounds.

21. Ibid.

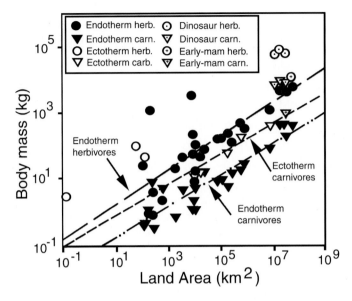

Fig. 1.7. Body masses of various animals (extinct or not) as a function of land area inhabited. The North American megafauna are evident as a cluster near the top right. From Gary P. Burness, Jared Diamond, and Timothy Flannery, "Dinosaurs, Dragons, and Dwarfs: The Evolution of Maximal Body Size," 14520. Reprinted with permission. Copyright 2001 National Academy of Sciences, USA.

The correlation between landmass and body size also explains many cases of small body size, in particular the numerous cases of dwarfism in animals that have become confined to islands. A classic case can be found on Wrangel Island in the Siberian Arctic. Rising sea levels separated this island from the mainland about twelve thousand years ago. The local mammoth population found itself stranded on a small landmass for which it was poorly suited. Evolution quickly (five thousand years is quick for evolution) remedied this imbalance by selecting for a size reduction of greater than 50 percent. Humans are not immune to this law of landmass and body size, as recently demonstrated by the discovery of prehistoric three-foot-tall humans who evolved on the small Indonesian island of Flores.[22] There are many other similar cases to be found in biology textbooks. On the other hand, North America is a large area, so it is to be expected that its animals would also be large.

Another likely factor in the large size of the megafauna was the need to keep warm, a particularly important factor during the ice ages. Large size in animals means a larger volume-to-surface-area ratio and hence an advantage in conserving heat. The relationships between body mass and structure or function are termed *allometrics,* a fascinating and vibrant field of biological inquiry beyond the scope of this discussion.

It has also been suggested that the evolution of large size in mammals was driven by increases in the concentration of oxygen in the atmosphere.[23] In the past 205 million years, the levels of oxygen in the atmosphere have increased from about 10 percent (by volume) to the current level of 21 percent. This correlates nicely with an increase in the body mass of mammals over geologic time and may be a consequence of the high energy demands of mammalian life history and the fact that larger animals require higher ambient oxygen levels to sustain maximal metabolic rates. Mammals in particular would have benefited from this higher level of oxygen because of the inherent inefficiency of oxygen transfer to the fetus as a consequence of placental reproduction.

22. See P. T. Brown et al., "A New Small-Bodied Hominid from the Late Pleistocene of Flores, Indonesia."

23. See Paul G. Falkowski et al., "The Risk of Oxygen over the Past 205 Million Years and the Evolution of Large Placental Mammals."

Last, what about those dinosaurs? Why were many of them so much bigger than even the Pleistocene megafauna? Ectothermy goes a good ways toward explaining this phenomenon if you are willing to accept that dinosaurs were cold-blooded, but many scientists now think dinosaurs may have been warm-blooded. An alternative explanation argues that some dinosaurs had a substantially larger plant-food base due to an elevated concentration of CO_2 in the atmosphere. Plants presumably responded with increased photosynthesis and productivity. More food, bigger animals. Determining the concentration of CO_2 in the long-ago atmosphere is a daunting task, but creditable reports estimate the level could have been >2,000 ppm (parts per million) from sixty to fifty-two million years ago, which compares to the current level of around 370 ppm.[24] If such high levels were present earlier, during the reign of dinosaurs, then dino-plants would have had prolific productivity.

So if big worked in the Pleistocene and before, why is small better now? Answer: us again, at least in some cases. Humans are a powerful selective force for small size in animals. Smaller sizes lead to shorter life cycles and earlier sexual maturity, which results in an improved ability to withstand the pressure of heavy predation. As an example, consider the case of the Atlantic cod, which has decreased markedly both in age and in size at maturation during the past three decades alone due to heavy fishing pressure by humans.[25] This rapid change apparently represents a true evolutionary adjustment, not just direct selection in which the bigger fish are removed.

---

24. See Paul N. Pearson and Martin R. Palmer, "Atmospheric Carbon Dioxide Concentrations over the Past 60 Million Years."

25. See S. Barot et al., "Long-Term Trend in the Maturation Reaction Norm of Two Cod Stocks."

Let's go back to the story of the disappearing giant sloths. Although many genera of sloths did disappear,[26] we do have two that managed to endure: *Bradypus,* the three-toed sloth, and *Choloepus,* the two-toed sloth. These animals have the traits that are typical of survivors of the megafaunal extinction: small body size (twenty pounds at best) and a habitat (treetops) that keeps them well separated from humans. About the only time that modern sloths come down from their tree perch is to defecate.

There are many other examples of the move toward smaller size and quicker maturity in response to human predation. Even the mighty bison underwent considerable dwarfing between 11,000 B.P. and 4,000 B.P. as the species readjusted to a new environment that included continuous hunting by Indians.[27] Quicker-maturing individuals were favored in the scheme of evolution since they could outreproduce larger, slow-to-mature individuals. Also, small animals were more agile and could get out of harm's way faster. Finally, it is reasonable to imagine that early humans (as with modern ones) would have been looking for the largest trophy to fill their pot or hang on the wall.

The bison story is a complicated one with many twists. Their near extirpation in the 1800s is usually seen as white man's folly, but it can also be seen as an unavoidable continuation of the forces that wiped out the megafauna. Even without the interference of white hunters in the 1800s, the bison might have been doomed anyway. The reintroduction of the horse into America by the Spaniards in the 1500s had shifted the equilibrium between the Indians and the bison. It is

26. The exact number is hard to pin down, but one source estimates that, worldwide, thirty-five genera of sloths disappeared (http://www.sloth-world.org/Sloth-FAQ.html).

27. Jerry N. McDonald, *North American Bison: Their Classification and Evolution,* 250.

at least feasible that the bison would have disappeared if this experiment had been allowed to run its course for a few more centuries.[28]

What might have been the fate of the Lewis and Clark Expedition if the megafauna had still been there? There are many scenarios, and I seriously invite you to suggest your own. The only way for the megafauna to still be around is if the Indians had never shown up. If you take the Indians out of the picture, then a lot of things would have been different for Lewis and Clark. They would have had plenty to eat, what with all those slow and naive ground sloths ambling around, so easy to kill. They were good enough woodsmen that they probably could have dealt with the weather and built their own shelters for the severe winters on the Great Plains. But the Corps of Discovery was highly dependent on the Indians for information on which rivers to follow and where to cross the mountains. Plus, the Indians provided them with horses, which were indispensable for hauling their supplies over the mountains. Without the Indians, the Expedition may have been defeated by the maze of mountains in Montana and Idaho. Or they might have wandered off course and ended up a long way from their goal. That is what happened to Mackenzie the first time he tried to cross Canada. His goal was the Pacific Ocean, but through a slight miscalculation he ended up at the Arctic Ocean instead. He had to try again later after he had brushed up on his navigational skills back in London.

The point of all this is that the ecosystems that Lewis and Clark found were far from free from human interference. In fact, the "natural" system had been replaced with one shaped largely by humans. The extinction of the megafauna literally opened the door for other

28. Dan Flores, "Bison Ecology and Bison Diplomacy: The Southern Plains from 1800 to 1850," 465.

mammals that had evolved to cope with humans in Asia to move in for the first time. These included practically all the big mammals that Lewis and Clark saw: elk, moose, plains bison, and grizzly bear. According to one view, the bison on the Great Plains were just a "weed species" that moved into the void left by the extinction of the megafauna.[29] There are no known fossils of grizzly bears in the contiguous United States before thirteen thousand years ago. Recent evidence from mitochondrial DNA from permafrost-preserved bears in Alaska has confirmed that these bears did not have a long history of isolation from the founding Asian population.[30] The grizzlies moved in to take over the ecological niche left open by the demise of the short-faced bear, which was about twice the weight of a modern grizzly. A bear of such dimensions would have been a formidable adversary when met on the open prairie with the limited firepower possessed by Lewis and Clark. Indeed, such encounters would likely have an outcome much less favorable than that described by Lewis on May 5, 1805:

> Capt. Clark and Drewyer killed the largest brown bear this evening which we have yet seen. it was a most tremendious looking anamal, and extreemly hard to kill notwithstanding he had five balls through his lungs and five others in various parts he swam more than half the distance across the river to a sandbar & it was at least twenty minutes before he died; he did not attempt to attact, but fled and made the most tremendous roaring from the moment he was shot.

---

29. Ibid.

30. See Jennifer A. Leonard, Robert K. Wayne, and Alan Cooper, "Population Genetics of Ice Age Brown Bears."

The next day, Lewis wrote further about their bear problems:

> I find that the curiossity of our party is pretty well satisfyed with rispect to this anamal, the formidable appearance of the male bear killed on the 5th added to the difficulty with which they die when even shot through the vital parts, has staggered the resolution several of them, others however seem keen for action with the bear; I expect these gentlemen will give us some amusement shotly as they soon begin now to coppolate.

His prediction proved true only a few days later, May 11:

> About 5 P.M. my attention was struck by one of the Party running at a distance towards us and making signs and hallowing as if in distress. I ordered the perogues to put to, and waited untill he arrived; I now found that it was Bratton. . . . [H]e arrived so much out of breath that it was several minutes before he could tell what had happened; . . . he had shot a brown bear which immediately turned on him and pursued him a considerable distance but he had wounded it so badly that it could not overtake him; I immediately turned out with seven of the party in quest of this monster, we at length found his trale and persued him about a mile by the blood through very thick brush of rosebushes and the large leafed willow; We finally found him concealed in some very thick brush and shot him through the skull with two balls; we proceeded [to] dress him as soon as possible, we found him in good order; it was a monstrous beast, not quite so large as that we killed a few days past but in all other rispects much the same the hair is remarkably long, fine, and rich, tho' he appears parshally to have discharged his winter coat; we now found that Bratton had shot him through the center of the lungs, notwithstanding which he had pursued him near half a mile and had returned more than double that

distance and with his talons had prepared himself a bed in the earth about 2 feet deep and five long and was perfectly alive when we found him which could not have been less than two hours after he received the wound; these bears, being so hard to die, reather intimedates us all; I must confess that I do not like the gentlemen and had rather fight two Indians than one bear.

Several themes thus emerge from these issues that are worth keeping in mind when considering the long-term view of nature in the West. The first is that prior to Lewis and Clark there was an astounding lack of understanding about what was out there with respect to both natural history and geography. The second, and perhaps more profound, concept is that nature is highly dynamic. Certainly, things have changed a lot since Lewis and Clark came through, but there were other equally dramatic changes much earlier that humans had a major hand in. The concept of the American West as unspoiled paradise prior to the 1800s is attractive, but it is misguided when viewed in a larger perspective of geologic time. Last, these pre-Euro-American changes raise complex questions for modern conservation biology and attempts to restore ecosystems in the West. Exactly how far back should we attempt to set the clock?

CHAPTER 2

❧

Flagship Species

L ewis and Clark discovered several new plants that stand out as particularly appropriate icons of the Expedition. Chief among these is certainly the two genera, *Lewisia* and *Clarkia,* that were named after the captains.[1] Following close behind is *Calochortus elegans* (cat's ear or elegant mariposa lily), which qualifies as symbolic because it represented a new genus that contains some of the most strikingly beautiful and varied plants in the West. Finally can be added *Philadelphus lewisii* (Lewis's mock orange) and *Mimulus lewisii* (Lewis's monkey-flower), partly for aesthetic reasons, but also because of the use of Lewis's name for the specific epithet *lewisii.* The events surrounding the origin of these names involve not only Lewis and Clark but also several other figures of historical note, especially Frederick Pursh,

1. Strictly speaking, only Lewis bore the official rank of captain, but he always referred to Clark by that rank, and the two men shared command on an equal footing. When Lewis recruited Clark for the Expedition, he offered Clark a commission as captain. Despite the support of Jefferson, Congress provided the official commission of only second lieutenant to the disappointment of both men.

a professional botanist hired to provide the formal descriptions. The strange sequence of events by which these names emerged provides an intriguing glimpse into the nexus of human personalities, fate, and the advance of science.

Lewisia and *Clarkia*

No plants are more representative of the spirit of discovery of the Lewis and Clark Expedition than are *Lewisia* (Lewis's bitterroot) and *Clarkia* (ragged robin or elkhorns). Both of these plants were new genera to science at the time. Finding a new genus is significant, as it was even back then, so these plants are well worth our attention. In the case of *Lewisia* there is considerably more to the story than just a pretty flower. The plant was an important source of food for Indians. The common name, bitterroot, provided the present-day names for a major mountain range and also one of the world's premier trout

Fig. 2.1. Bitterroot (*Lewisia rediviva*). Photo by Keith Karoly.

Fig. 2.2. *Lewisia cotyledon*, a highly variable and widely cultivated plant native to the Klamath and Siskiyou mountain ranges in southwestern Oregon. Photo by Keith Karoly.

streams. The physiology and ecology of this plant also provide some interesting scientific features. Finally, the various species of *Lewisia* are of great horticultural interest today because of their incredible beauty and variety (figs. 2.1–2.4). There is a whole cult of *Lewisia* enthusiasts who grow and sell different species of *Lewisia,* and several books have been written on just this genus. *Lewisia* is especially popular with European gardeners.

Lewis first described bitterroot on August 22, 1805, as the party was camped just east of what are today called the Bitterroot Mountains:

> The parts were brittle, hard, of the size of a small quill, cilindric and as white as snow throughout, except some small parts of the hard black rind which they had not seperated in the preperation. this the Indians with me informed were always boiled for use. I made the exp[e]rement, found that they became perfectly soft by boiling, but had a very bitter taste, which was naucious to my pallate, and transfered them to the Indians who had eat them heartily.

Fig. 2.3. *Lewisia tweedyi*, an uncommon plant from the Wenatchee Mountains of central Washington. Some authorities now place this species in the genus *Cistanthe*. Photo by Burl Mostul of Rare Plant Research.

The plant is common in Montana and was relied on heavily for food by the Indians. Apparently, the name bitterroot was well earned, but the Indians liked it well enough. This plant is so nutritious that it supplies about thirteen hundred Calories per hour of collection time and consequently could, when in season, easily provide a large portion of daily nutritional needs. Bitterroot was so prized as a foodstuff that a grain sack full of cleaned and dried roots was considered by the Indians to be a fair trade for a good horse.[2]

2. See Kevin T. Jones and David B. Madsen, "Further Experiments in Native Food Procurement."

Fig. 2.4. *Lewisia leeana* from Onion Mountain in southwestern Oregon.
Copyright 2007 Mark Turner.

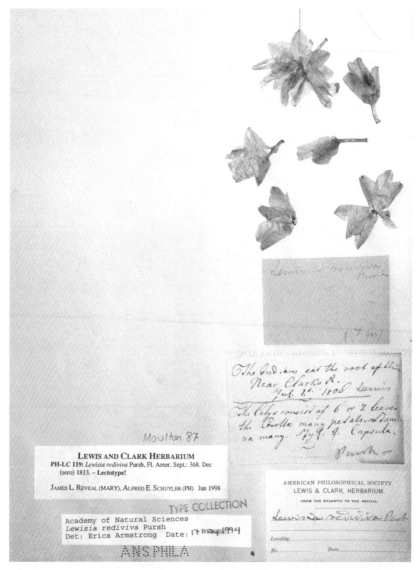

Fig. 2.5. The original specimen of *Lewisia rediviva* from the Lewis and Clark Herbarium. Botany Department, Academy of Natural Sciences, Philadelphia.

Lewis's initial encounter was with dried roots only, but he came upon the flower the following spring when camped at Traveller's Rest on the Bitterroot River just east of the Rocky Mountains. At that time, Lewis recognized the plant as the same one that provided him with the bitter roots the previous summer. As was his habit, he collected some samples (including flower, stem, and roots) and dried them in his plant press for return to Philadelphia for the experts to sort through (fig. 2.5). Herein lies one of the more interesting tales pertaining to this plant. Upon their return to Philadelphia in 1807, the specimens were given to Bernard McMahon, a prominent gardener, seedsman, and nurseryman. McMahon noticed a curious thing. The dried plants were beginning to sprout new green growth. McMahon, being an experienced gardener, coaxed them into growth and then displayed them in his store. Frederick Pursh, the professional botanist from Germany, was assigned the task of cataloging and describing the plants that Lewis and Clark brought back. Pursh provided the scientific name we know today, honoring Lewis in the genus name, *Lewisia,* and the ability to return to life in the specific epithet (*rediviva* means "restored to life"). The phenomenal hardiness of *L. rediviva* was demonstrated again with a specimen, collected decades later by David Douglas, that flowered after being shipped to Kew Gardens in London. This particular specimen had been immersed in boiling water and then dried for eighteen months before it revived.[3] This amazing ability to resprout is a consequence of some unusual physiology of this remarkable plant.

There are sixteen species of *Lewisia,* and they are found only in western North America.[4] The family to which they belong—the

3. Roy C. Eliott, *The Genus* Lewisia, 53.
4. See Flora of North America Editorial Committee, eds., *Flora of North America North of Mexico.*

purslane family (Portulacaceae)—is widespread in temperate zones and has many edible species, including purslane, miner's lettuce, and spring beauty. The next sentence following Lewis's initial description of bitterroot (quoted above) mentions another plant in the purslane family (*Claytonia lanceolata*) with tuberlike roots that

> were about the size of a nutmeg, and of an irregularly rounded form. . . . [T]hese I also boiled agreeably to the instruction of the Indians and found them very agreeable. they resemble the Jerusalem Artichoke very much in their flavor and I thought them preferable, however there is some allowance to be made for the length of time I have now been without vegitable food to which I was always much attatched. these are certainly the best root I have yet seen in uce among the Indians.

Plants in the genus (*Claytonia*) have been called "fairy spuds" by the late Euell Gibbons, a modern-day guru of wild foods. They are among the most delightful and flavorful of wild foods, the only drawback being their small size.

Many species of *Lewisia* are remarkable in that they grow only in the harshest, driest, most sun-blasted sites imaginable, appropriately called "moonscapes." Typically, they may be found on gravel flats or stony cliffs where few other plants can survive. As such, they are truly representative of the harsh and arid environment of the American West and thus appropriately considered the flagship plant of the Lewis and Clark Expedition.

The amazing ability of *Lewisia* to thrive in dry environments is largely a consequence of their unique mode of photosynthesis. In order to obtain CO_2 for photosynthesis, all plants must open the pores (stomata) in their leaves. Whenever they do so, though, they risk losing water through the process of transpiration. *Lewisia* are good at avoiding water loss due in part to their thick, succulent leaves that store water in much the same way as a cactus. Even more remarkably, *Lewisia* open their leaf pores at night to take in CO_2 when the risk of water loss is minimal. The pores are then closed during the day when there is the highest danger of water loss due to high temperatures. The plants are doing part of their photosynthesis at night—something of a contradiction, since by definition photosynthesis is driven by light energy. However, it is possible to take up CO_2 at night and store it in chemical form such that the CO_2 can be released later the next day and then converted into sugars by that part of photosynthesis that requires light energy. This specialized mode of photosynthesis is known as CAM photosynthesis, short for Crassulacean Acid Metabolism, since it is a common feature in plants in the family Crassulaceae.

In addition to succulent leaves and CAM photosynthesis, *Lewisia* has another trick for dealing with drought. The plant is active only during the spring months and completely dormant the rest of the year, when weather conditions are either too cold or too dry. From late spring through fall, there are no aboveground parts present, only roots. Bitterroot has taken this lifestyle to the extreme. It survives only in conditions where there is almost no summer rain, making it something of a challenge for gardeners.

Upon their return east, members of the Corps of Discovery were obliged to spend nearly four weeks along the Clearwater River in western Idaho while they waited for the snow to melt enough for them to cross the rugged mountains. This gave them ample opportunity to botanize. About one-quarter of all the specimens in the Lewis and Clark Herbarium were collected in Idaho on the return trip. Notable among these plants was elkhorns or ragged robin (*Clarkia pulchella*). The name *Clarkia* was provided nearly eight years later by Pursh (fig. 2.6). Pursh's description, based on Lewis's original comments, reads: "A beautifull herbaceous plant from the Kooskooskee [Clearwater] & Clarks R." Pursh also assigned the specific epithet of *pulchella*, which means "beautiful."

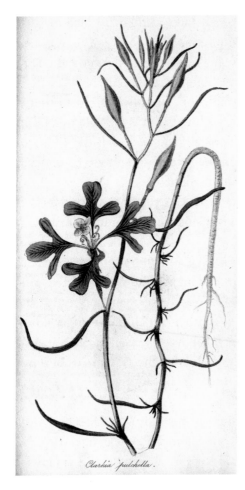

Fig. 2.6. *Clarkia pulchella*, as illustrated by Pursh in his 1813 publication, *Flora Americae Septentrionalis.* Copyright American Philosophical Society.

Lewis went into great technical detail in his description of this flower. Paul Cutright includes Lewis's whole description because it is such a good example of Lewis's mastery of botanical terminology. For instance, Lewis correctly used the following terms: *radix, villose, sessile, obtusely, calyx, corolla, superior/inferior, stamens, filaments, anthers, pistillum, style, stigma,* and *monopetalous.*[5]

5. Cutright, *Lewis and Clark,* 298.

Fig. 2.7. *Clarkia pulchella* (elkhorns). Photo by Keith Karoly.

There are about forty-one species of *Clarkia* in the West, all of striking beauty.[6] The flowers have an unusual feature in that the stigma (the pollen-receptive surface) has four petal-like lobes, thus giving the appearance of a tiny white flower embedded within a larger pink one (fig. 2.7). *Clarkia* is prized by gardeners around the world, though this genus has not generated the same enthusiasm from horticulturists as have *Lewisia* and *Calochortus.*

Lewis's ability to deal with technical botany reflects back to Jefferson's wisdom in forging the Expedition. As you can imagine, trained botanists were rare in colonial America. At that time, there was only one textbook written on botany by an American, *Elements of Botany* (1803) by Benjamin Barton of Philadelphia. Jefferson was a close confidant of Barton, so he recruited Barton's help to bring Lewis's botanical training up to an acceptable level.

Jefferson fully recognized the importance of botany, as evidenced in his writings. For instance, in a letter to Thomas Cooper in 1814, he wrote:

> Botany I rank with the most valuable sciences, whether we consider its subjects as furnishing the principal subsistence of life to man and beast, delicious varieties for our tables, refreshments from our orchards, the adornments of our flower-borders, shade and perfume of our groves, materials for our buildings, or medicaments for our bodies. . . . No country gentleman should be without what amuses every step he takes into his fields.[7]

From the earliest days of planning for the Expedition, Jefferson had botany in mind as a chief objective. He even recruited the prominent French botanist André Michaux to lead an expedition to

---

6. See James C. Hickman, *The Jepson Manual: Higher Plants of California.*

7. Andrew A. Lipscomb and Albert E. Bergh, *The Writings of Thomas Jefferson,* 14:201.

explore the West. That venture, conceived ten years before Lewis and Clark's, ran afoul of international politics and never got west of Kentucky, but the basic idea was in place and evolved in Jefferson's mind until it eventually reached fruition in 1803.

When the time came for Jefferson to pick a leader for the Expedition, he wanted to be sure that botany was included somewhere in the package. Lewis was a near fit but needed a little fine-tuning, as is evident in Jefferson's letter to Barton from February 27, 1803:

> It was impossible to find a character who to a compleat science in botany, natural history, mineralogy & astronomy, joined the firmness of constitution & character, prudence, habits adapted to the woods, & a familiarity with the Indian manners & character, requisite for this undertaking. All the latter qualifications Capt. Lewis has. Altho' no regular botanist &c. he possesses a remarkable store of accurate observation on all the subjects of the three kingdoms, & will therefore readily single out whatever presents itself new to him in either: and he has qualified himself for taking those observations of longitude & latitude necessary to fix the geography of the line he passes through. In order to draw his attention at once to the objects most desirable, I must ask the favor of you to prepare for him a note of those in lines of botany, zoology, or of Indian history which you think most worthy of inquiry & observation. He will be with you in Philadelphia in two or three weeks, & will wait on you, and receive thankfully on paper, and any verbal communications which you may be so good as to make to him. I make no apology for this trouble, because I know that the same wish to promote science which has induced me to bring forward this proposition, will induce you to aid in promoting it. Accept assurances of my friendly esteem & high respect.[8]

8. Jackson, *Letters of the Expedition*, 16.

Barton became so intrigued with the prospects for this venture that he wanted to go himself. It almost happened, but eventually he settled on just providing the instruction that Jefferson requested. That is probably just as well, since Barton was thirty-seven years old, middle-aged by the standards of the day, and would have certainly fared poorly on such an arduous trip. Lewis proved to be an exceptional student and absorbed an impressive amount of knowledge, including how to preserve specimens (either plant, bird, or mammal); the importance of proper labeling, including place and date of collection; and the fundamentals of the Linnaean system for classifying specimens with Latin names. Lewis also carried Barton's textbook with him all the way to Oregon and back, eventually returning it to Barton with a note of thanks inscribed. Jefferson tried to enlist Barton to publish the descriptions of the plant specimens brought back by the Expedition, but, strangely, Barton never came through, and the opportunity passed on to the young, ambitious Pursh instead.

Calochortus (Mariposa Lily)

A SPOTLESS SOUL, PLANT SAINT, THAT EVERY ONE MUST LOVE AND SO BE MADE BETTER. IT PUTS THE WILDEST MOUNTAINEER ON HIS GOOD BEHAVIOUR. WITH THIS PLANT THE WHOLE WORLD WOULD SEEM RICH THOUGH NONE OTHER EXISTED.

—John Muir in reference to *Calochortus*,
in *Our National Parks*

Calochortus is the third and last new genus named by Pursh from the Lewis and Clark collection. The herbarium label is dated May 17, 1806, and bears Pursh's comments, copied from Lewis's original

Fig. 2.8. Elegant mariposa lily (*Calochortus elegans*) from southwestern Oregon. Photo by Keith Karoly.

notes: "A Small bulb of a pleasant flavour, eat by the natives. On the Kooskooske (Clearwater)."

Calochortus stands out as especially remarkable in part because of its great beauty. *C. elegans* is sometimes called elegant cat's ear lily because the petals, with their soft, fuzzy hairs on the inner surface, do indeed resemble a cat's ear (fig. 2.8). The specimen collected by Lewis on May 17, 1806, was used by Pursh to describe a new genus whose name was taken from the Greek *kalos* (beautiful) and *chortos* (grass). It is not a grass (it is usually considered to be in the lily family, as Pursh surely recognized), but it certainly is extraordinarily beautiful (see figs. 2.9 and 2.10). Some modern botanists have placed *Calochortus* in a family of its own (Calochortaceae), but this is not universally accepted. Nowadays, authorities recognize at least seventy-one species of *Calochortus*,[9] with a widespread distribution

9. See Frank Callahan, "The Genus *Calochortus*."

Fig. 2.9. Sagebrush mariposa lily (*Calochortus macrocarpus*) from along the Columbia River in Okanogan County, Washington. Photo by Keith Karoly.

Fig. 2.10. Wide-fruited mariposa lily (*Calochortus eurycarpus*) from Baker County, Oregon. Copyright 2007 Mark Turner.

from British Columbia to Mexico and as far east as the Dakotas, with the diversity centered in California (fig. 2.11). The flowers of *Calochortus* are found in a striking variety of forms, including large tuliplike blossoms (mariposa lily and star tulips), open-faced flowers with hairy petals (cat's ears, such as *C. elegans*), and nodding, bell-shaped flowers (fairy lanterns). Gardeners have long been attracted to the beauty of *Calochortus*. A number of nurseries, especially in California, specialize in selling the bulbs.

Calochortus is a large and complex genus that has attracted the attention of taxonomically inclined botanists for many years. Marion Ownbey, a prominent American plant taxonomist, once wrote a 189-page monograph devoted solely to this genus. Ownbey also gave witness to the high food value of the bulbs, which he found to be "crisp and starchy, and taste not unlike an ordinary potato tuber." More recently, botanists Thomas Patterson and Thomas Givnish at the University of Wisconsin have reexamined the complex relatedness among the many species of *Calochortus* by using modern molecular techniques.[10]

Whereas scientists such as Ownbey relied primarily on floral morphology to determine relationships, it is now possible to gain further insight into such issues by comparisons of DNA sequences. The stereotypical image of the gentle botanist hunched over a hand lens while teasing apart a tiny flower is somewhat dated, replaced by the, one hopes, still gentle botanist hunched over a computer monitor staring at A's, T's, G's, and C's. Patterson and Givnish compared the sequences of chloroplast DNA of practically all species of *Calochortus* and fine-tuned our understanding of the relatedness between

10. Ownbey, "A Monograph of the Genus *Calochortus*," 384; Patterson and Givnish, "Geographic Cohesion, Chromosomal Evolution, Parallel Adaptive Radiations, and Consequent Floral Adaptations in *Calochortus* (Calochortaceae): Evidence from a cpDNA Phylogeny."

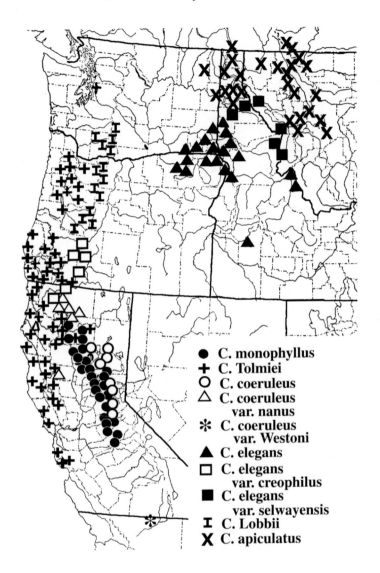

● C. monophyllus
+ C. Tolmiei
○ C. coeruleus
△ C. coeruleus
   var. nanus
✳ C. coeruleus
   var. Westoni
▲ C. elegans
□ C. elegans
   var. creophilus
■ C. elegans
   var. selwayensis
Ɪ C. Lobbii
X C. apiculatus

Fig. 2.11. The distribution of several species of *Calochortus* showing the restricted geographical distribution that is typical for species in this genus. From Ownbey, "Monography of *Calochortus*," 384. Copyright1940 Missouri Botanical Garden.

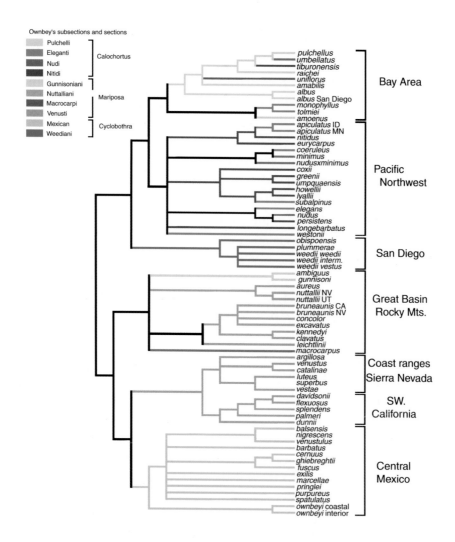

Fig. 2.12. A phylogenetic tree showing the relationships among the various species of *Calochortus*. The degree of relatedness was based on chloroplast DNA sequence. The colors indicate the groupings as determined earlier based on floral morphology. From Patterson and Givnish, "Geographic Cohesion," 256. Reprinted with permission. Copyright 2003 *New Phytologist*.

the various species (fig. 2.12). For the most part, Ownbey's original groupings have held up well.

One does not need to be a technical expert to deduce from figure 2.12 that *Calochortus* is indeed a rich and varied genus, with many species scattered throughout western North America. The genus is a great example of adaptive radiation, a favorite topic with biologists going back to Darwin. The basic idea is that many different species can arise from a common ancestor, given enough time and sufficient isolation so as to prevent exchange of genes. Classic examples are the many species of finches and tortoises on the Galápagos Islands that Darwin used as a central argument for the theory of evolution. In the case of *Calochortus,* the genetic isolation comes from the mountainous terrain in the American West and from the large seeds that are not easily dispersed. Also contributing to the genetic isolation is the fastidiousness with which many species cling to particular soil types. The various species of *Calochortus* probably started to diverge from each other about seven million years ago. All of them were unknown to science until Lewis made his collection of *C. elegans* in 1806, and then the botanical floodgates were opened.

As if attempting to catch the spirit of the West in botanical form, different species of *Calochortus* can be found in deserts, grasslands, montane woodlands, seasonal pools, meadows, and forest understories. Most of these species are restricted to small geographic areas, and several are so rare as to be endangered. At least eighteen species (including *C. elegans*) are tolerant of serpentine soils. These are soils that are the ultimate expression of the essence of the American West in the sense of the harsh, barren, and bleak conditions they provide for plants as a consequence of mineral imbalances of the bedrock material (fig. 2.13).

The name "serpentine" is somewhat misleading, since it has no reptilian implication other than the fact that the parent bedrock ma-

Fig. 2.13. View of undisturbed serpentine areas (*right of center*) in the Klam-ath Mountains of southern Oregon showing typical sparse vegetation. The adjacent area (*left of center*) is an undisturbed forest on normal granitic soils without the mineral imbalances of serpentine soils. Photo by author.

terial (peridotite or serpentinite) has snaky streaks of mineral swirls. A comparable but somewhat more descriptive term is "ultramafic soil," which correctly though cryptically indicates that the soils are high in *ma*gnesium and iron (*ferr*ic). Serpentine soils are low in essential elements such as nitrogen, phosphorous, calcium, and potassium and, at the same time, high in toxic elements such as nickel and chromium. Sites with serpentine soils invariably have anemic, spindly vegetation. You might think that botanists would shy away from serpentine areas, but actually botanists flock to them because they support a large number of rare and endemic species. Some of the greatest botanical diversity in North America can be found in serpentine areas such as the Klamath and Siskiyou Mountains of southern Oregon and northern California.[11]

That such spectacular and widespread plants as the various species of *Calochortus* could have escaped the attention of science prior to Lewis and Clark's discovery is a good indication of the general state of ignorance about the natural history of the American West at the time. Pursh had only one withered specimen to work with, so he had no way of knowing how diverse and widespread this genus was in the West. Had he known, it seems reasonable to imagine that he would have given it a more significant name—such as *Clarkia*, which of course he assigned to another plant. What became known as *Clarkia* is certainly an attractive plant, but the name *Clarkia* might have been more appropriately used for *Calochortus*, since the latter is more widespread, was an important food plant of the Natives as well as Lewis and Clark themselves, and symbolizes so much of the spirit of the West, including a predilection for dry, harsh sites and the conflict between stark surroundings and beauty, grace, and function. Pursh got it right in selecting the name for *Lewisia*, which works well as a symbol for the Lewis and Clark Expedition, but he missed a great chance for a second winner with *Clarkia/Calochortus*.

Philadelphus lewisii (Lewis's Mock Orange)

The showy shrub mock orange is a worthy symbol of the Expedition for a number of reasons: its abundance along western rivers, the specific epithet that Pursh attached, and its status as the state flower of Idaho (fig. 2.14). The genus was not a new one, having been long known from Eurasia and from the eastern United States. The name

11. See David R. Wallace, *The Klamath Knot.*

Fig. 2.14. Lewis's mock orange (*Philadelphus lewisii*) blossoms and foliage from the Columbia Gorge, Washington. Copyright 2007 Mark Turner.

of the genus might suggest a connection to the city that played such a big role in the planning and preparation for the Expedition, but regrettably that story does not hold up. The genus was named by Linnaeus to honor Ptolemy Philadelphus (36–12 B.C.), king of Egypt and the youngest child of Mark Antony and Cleopatra.

In Idaho, this plant often goes by the common name syringa. It does indeed bear superficial resemblance to lilac (whose genus is *Syringa*), but this is misleading since lilacs and mock oranges are in different families (the Hydrangeaceae, or hydrangea, family for mock orange and the Oleaceae, or olive, family for lilac) and thus are not closely related. The names become even more confusing when considering that the term *syringa* is based on the Greek word meaning "pipe" in reference to the hollow stems that ancient Persians used for their pipes. The term was originally applied (by Linnaeus) to *Philadelphus* even though the generic name *Syringa* eventually ended up on a different plant. This unfortunate and confusing nomenclatural morass can be resolved with a simple rule: as long as you are dealing with native shrubs in the western United States, mock orange = syringa = *Philadelphus lewisii*.

There is less obfuscation surrounding the name "mock orange." The blossoms have a strong and pleasant odor that is reminiscent of oranges. Once you learn this distinctive fragrance, it is often possible to know that you are in the vicinity of a patch of mock orange before you see it. The petals have been used to scent water since the time of the ancient Persians, but Lewis and Clark did not witness this practice, partly because *Philadelphus lewisii* is not as strongly fragrant as other species of mock orange.

Mimulus lewisii (Lewis's Monkey-flower)

Pursh also named the attractive flower *Mimulus lewisii* after Lewis when he published *Flora Americae Septentrionalis* (*The Flora of North America;* see Chapter 3). The original specimen has not been located. Pursh's description of the location ("the head springs of the Missouri, at the foot of Portage hill") where it was collected is somewhat cryptic but clearly refers to the area around Lemhi Pass where the Corps of Discovery passed in August 1805. Neither Lewis nor anyone else apparently had the inclination to mention their encounter with this plant in their journals. That is remarkable considering the incredible beauty of this flower.

Linnaeus had earlier named the genus *Mimulus* based on the diminutive of *mimus* (a mimic actor) in reference to the masklike appearance of the flowers. This plant has at least three features that make it one of most impressive flowers in the western United States.

First is the striking beauty of the pinkish-purple blossoms with their yellow-streaked throats. Second is their habitat, which is often alongside crystal-clear creeks or small waterfalls in montane forests, a fortuitous circumstance that adds even more to the inherent beauty of the blossom. In the Cascade Mountains of Washington and Oregon, *M. lewisii* often forms extensive stands in wet alpine meadows (fig. 2.15). Finally, the flowers have a delightful, sweet smell that is somehow powerful but not overwhelming.

The distinctive yellow throat patch in *Mimulus lewisii* is a key feature in its ability to attract bumblebees for pollination. The color is due to a brilliant carotenoid pigment that apparently is close to irresistible for bumblebees. Bees see colors differently than we do. Ultraviolet colors, invisible to us, are strong beacons to bees and help them to home in on their floral targets. The importance of this visual cue in *M. lewisii* was demonstrated recently in a comparative study between this species and its sister species, *Mimulus cardinalis*.[12] The latter species is strikingly red, a color that bees are generally indifferent toward. Instead, *M. cardinalis* is pollinated by hummingbirds. Although they are capable of interbreeding, they remain reproductively isolated due to their different modes of pollination. The yellow throat color of *M. lewisii* is controlled by a gene or set of genes at one discrete location (a "quantitative trait locus") called yellow upper (YUP, for short) on a chromosome. With scientists playing the role of artificial pollinator, it was possible to produce hybrids and backcrosses between these two species in which the YUP form ("allele") of *M. lewisii* was switched with the corresponding allele (YUP) from *M. cardinalis*. Such artificial pollination is routinely accomplished in the greenhouse by use of a "bee stick" in which a dead bee is glued

12. See H. D. Bradshaw and Douglas W. Schemske, "Allele Substitution at a Flower Color Locus Produces a Pollinator Shift in Monkeyflowers."

Fig. 2.15. *Mimulus lewisii* in wet high-elevation meadow in the Oregon
Cascade Range. Photo by Keith Karoly.

Fig. 2.16. A, wild-type *Mimulus lewisii;* C, *M. cardinalis;* and the corresponding crossbred progeny in which the YUP allele was switched. From Bradshaw and Schemske, "Allele Substitution," 177. Copyright 2003 *Nature.*

to a stick and then used to manually collect pollen for transfer to another blossom. The tiny hairs on a bee's body are perfectly suited to pick up tiny pollen grains. The result was a *M. lewisii* flower lacking its distinct yellow throat patch and a *M. cardinalis* flower with diminished red color (fig. 2.16). This switching of a single allele led to predictable confusion on the part of pollinators. Hummingbirds now seemed at least partially inclined to visit *M. lewisii,* and bumblebees were similarly misled to *M. cardinalis.* Such studies help scientists not only understand the importance of color for pollination but also, more fundamentally, reveal how a single mutation might be involved in shifting pollinator preference and thus the directions of floral evolution and formation of new species.

Mimulus has emerged as such a valuable model for studying plant evolution and speciation that several species (including *M. lewisii*) are now the target of an extensive genome sequencing project funded by the National Science Foundation for more than four million dollars. Much genetic information, including gene sequences and maps, is available at http://www.mimulusevolution.org.

CHAPTER 3

Missed Opportunities

When Lewis and Clark returned to Philadelphia they expected to enlist the aid of Benjamin Barton, the most prominent botanist in the United States and the author of the first American textbook on that subject, to catalog and describe their rich bounty of plant specimens. Barton had trained Lewis before the Expedition left and was the logical choice to provide the technical follow-up that the specimens required. Despite his good intentions, either his health or his resolve (no one seems to be sure which) began to waver, and the task fell to Frederick Pursh, who happened to be in town working as a collector for Barton. Furthermore, Pursh was a boarder at the home of Bernard McMahon, a Philadelphia nursery-man and seed merchant with whom both Jefferson and Lewis were well acquainted. When McMahon heard that the Lewis and Clark collection was in need of professional attention, he wrote to Lewis to recommend Pursh, who, in his opinion, "is better acquainted with plants in general than any man I ever conversed with on the subject."[1] Lewis accepted this advice and engaged Pursh for the work,

---

1. Jackson, *Letters of the Expedition*, 398.

paying him seventy dollars for his services.[2] Pursh worked on the collection for more than a year.

Meanwhile, Barton continued to struggle with failing health, Lewis went off to Louisiana to serve as governor, and Jefferson was apparently distracted by his other interests. Everyone expected that Lewis would eventually produce a natural history volume as well as the journal itself, both of which were eagerly anticipated, especially by Jefferson. Unfortunately, for reasons that have puzzled scholars ever since, Lewis could not bring himself to get the job done. A key factor was certainly Lewis's vulnerability to episodes of depression, of which Jefferson was well aware. The natural letdown after the completion of the Expedition, his poor luck in romance, the daunting scope of the project at hand, and the pressures of his administrative responsibilities (for which he was poorly suited) have all been suggested as contributing to Lewis's failure. For whatever reasons, no scientific write-up for the collection was forthcoming. Lewis's suicide in 1809 left the project without a central driving figure.

Although Pursh continued to work on the collection, his relationship with Barton began to sour, and he moved on to a new position as gardener for the Elgin Botanic Garden in New York.[3] Although Barton lived for six more years, he never published anything about the collection. Pursh's employment in the United States ended in 1811, and he returned to Europe. He took with him his notes and drawings and about one-quarter of the collection. He used this material to prepare his book titled *Flora Americae Septentrionalis* (*The Flora of North America*) in 1813 in which 130 of the plants from the Expedition were finally described for posterity. Most of Pursh's specimens eventually found their way back to Philadelphia where they were tucked away at the Academy of Natural Sciences. Years

2. Cutright, *Lewis and Clark,* 359.
3. James L. Reveal, "Making Drawings and Writing Descriptions," n.p.

Table 3.1. Partial list of plants collected by Lewis and Clark later reassigned to a new genus

Common name	Genus assigned by Pursh	Modern genus and species
Balsamroot	*Buphthalmum*	*Balsamorhiza sagittata*
Camas	*Phalangium*	*Camassia quamash*
Bitterbrush	*Tigarea*	*Purshia tridentata*
Oregon grape	*Berberis*	*Mahonia* or *Berberis* (three species)
Biscuitroot	*Seseli, Smyrnium*	*Lomatium nudicaule, L. triternatum*
Bear-grass	*Helonias*	*Xerophyllum tenax*

later, in 1896, the botanist for the academy, one Thomas Meehan, began to wonder where the other three-quarters of the collection might be. He eventually located the missing samples across town at the American Philosophical Society, "probably untouched for three-quarters of a century and somewhat decimated by beetles."[4] The rediscovery of the samples led to further documentation and careful preservation. Today, they are recognized as a monumental scientific and national treasure.

Pursh was a highly competent botanist whose work has held up well to the test of time, but later botanists have decided that several of the plants that Pursh described were actually distinct enough to deserve being elevated to the status of a new genus (table 3.1). Although Pursh did create the three new genera described in the previous chapter, he could just as well have created numerous other new genera from the samples returned by the Expedition.

4. Moulton, *Journals of the Expedition*, 12:6; Richard M. McCourt and Earle E. Spamer, "The Botanical Legacy of Lewis and Clark: The Most Famous Collection You Never Heard Of."

Although Pursh was meticulous, he was perhaps a bit too cautious in this regard. Yet it is hard to find fault, especially considering the large number of samples that Pursh had to work with, the poor condition of many of the specimens, and the fledgling state of the science of botany at that time. The six plants in table 3.1 are worthy of further consideration because they are all prominent in western landscapes and played significant roles in the Lewis and Clark Expedition and in the lives of Native peoples. There are at least fifteen additional examples of plants in which Pursh's name for the genus was later changed.[5] Although each of these additional plants has its own story, the plants themselves are generally less well known or abundant, and so they are not included here.

Balsamorhiza (Balsamroot)

Arrowleaf balsamroot (*Balsamorhiza sagittata*) was first collected on April 14, 1806, as the Expedition passed along the Columbia River in present-day Skamania or Klickitat County, Washington. Clark wrote that he "met Several parties of women and boys in Serch of herbs & roots to Subsist on maney of them had parcels of the Stems of the Sun flower."

Arrowleaf balsamroot does indeed resemble sunflower (the genus *Helianthus*) with its large bright-yellow flowers. Both plants are in the same family (Compositae, also called Asteraceae). However, true sunflowers generally bloom later in the summer and have dry, inedible stems. A further distinction for the botanically enlightened is that balsamroot flowers lack a pappus (a modified calyx), a most unusual state of affairs for plants in this family. This bit of botanical

---

5. See James L. Reveal, Gary E. Moulton, and Alfred E. Schuyler, "The Lewis and Clark Collections of Vascular Plants."

trivia is worth some reflection, because it can give us a glimpse into Lewis's botanical insight. Chances are pretty good that you do not know what a calyx is, unless you happen to have majored in botany in college. The percentage of the population in 1800 who could define a calyx was probably even less than today's, but Lewis knew. He used the term (though somewhat loosely) several times in the journals when providing technical descriptions of flowers. A calyx is the collective term for all the sepals of a flower. If that does not help, the sepals are the outermost ring of petal-like appendages in a flower, often seen as small green flaps outside of the petals. Most plants in the sunflower family have a pappus, which is a modified calyx, though you might need a hand lens to see it clearly. The feathery hairs on a dandelion seed are a typical pappus (fig. 3.1). You will not find anything like that on balsamroot.

Pursh's location and habitat statement in *Flora Americae Septentrionalis* reads as follows: "On dry barren hills, in the Rocky-mountains . . . Flowers large, yellow. The natives eat the young stems as they spring up, raw." The habitat is open hillsides and prairies at low to moderate elevations east of the Cascade Mountains. It is common and striking among open stands of sagebrush.

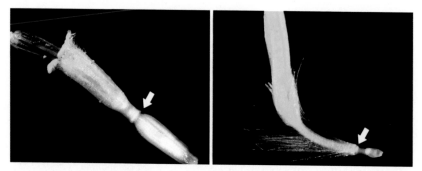

Fig. 3.1. The individual flowers (florets) of arrowleaf balsamroot (*left*) and dandelion (*right*), showing the absence of a pappus or modified calyx on the former. Photo by author.

All parts of the plant are edible, including stems, leaves, and seeds, but the roots, which are large, woody, and difficult to dig, are the most valuable, because they are loaded with a carbohydrate called inulin (see next section on camas).

Cooking the roots required a bit of work. The roots were peeled by pounding them to remove the outer bark and then cooked in a rock pit for twenty-four hours or longer, after which they could be eaten directly or dried for storing or trade. If cooked correctly, the roots can be quite sweet, so they were eaten as a treat or dessert. Although the Indians ate a lot of balsamroot, it apparently was not a major feature of the diet of the Expedition, which is probably a good thing, since balsamroot is similar (nutritionally and taxonomically) to Jerusalem artichokes, which have some undesirable properties, as described by John Gerard, one of England's pioneer planters of the early 1600s: "But in my judgement, which way soever they be drest and eaten they stir up and cause a filthie loathesome stinking winde with the bodie, thereby causing the belly to bee much pained and tormented, and are a meat more fit for swine, than men."[6] Despite these drawbacks, balsamroot served the Indians well, since, once cooked, it was a good source of energy (395 Cal 100 g^{-1}) and dietary fiber (250 g kg^{-1}).[7]

Camassia (Camas)

Camas is another example of the combination of great beauty and utility that graces many of the plants that the Expedition encountered (fig. 3.2). The men were near starvation as they made their way

---

6. *Gerard's Herbal,* quoted in A. Davidson, *The Oxford Companion to Food.*

7. M. P. Mullin et al., "Macronutrients Content of Yellow Glacier Lily and Balsamroot: Root Vegetables Used by Indigenous Peoples of Northwestern North America."

Fig. 3.2. Common camas (*Camassia quamash*) along the Columbia River, Washington. Copyright 2007 Mark Turner.

over Lolo Pass and down along the Clearwater River in present-day Idaho. As Clark noted, "The road through this hilley Countrey is verry bad passing."

Their travel was slowed by thick dog-hair stands of pine and other conifers, with large amounts of fallen timber that blocked their passage. They were cursed by truly wretched weather. Temperatures in the teens in the Bitterroot Valley were followed by days of rain and snow as they made their way through the Bitterroot and Clearwater Mountains. The journals are filled with an uncharacteristic flavor of pessimism. Progress required "the greatest exertion" (Clark). "The men without socks raped rags on their feet" (Whitehouse, a private who also kept a journal).

On September 16, they awoke to eight inches of new snow. With no food in camp, they set off through "the most terrible mountains I ever beheld" (Patrick Gass, a sergeant who also kept a journal). Clark wrote, "I have never been wet and as cold in every part as I ever was in my life, indeed I was at one time fearfull my feet would freeze in the thin mockersons which I wore."

Game was practically nonexistent. At one point, the men were so famished they killed one of their colts to eat. Imagine their great relief when they finally stumbled on some Nez Perce lodges as the terrain began to flatten out into the prairies of western Idaho. The Indians generously provided food to the starving party, but most of what they had available was camas root.

Clark, on September 20, 1805, described how the Indians prepared camas roots for consumption:

> Emence quantity of the quawmash or Pas-shi-co root gathered
> & in piles about the plains, those roots grow much an onion in
> marshy places the seed are in triangular Shell on the Stalk. they
> Sweat them in the following manner i.e. dig a large hole 3 feet
> deep Cover the bottom with Split wood on the top of which

they lay Small Stones of about 3 or 4 Inches thick, a Second layer of Splitted wood & Set the whole on fire which heats the Stones, after the fire is extinguished they lay grass & mud mixed on the Stones, on that dry grass which Supports the Pash-Shi-co root a thin Coat of the Same grass is laid on the top, a Small fire is kept when necessary in the Center of the kile &c.

After several days, the pit was uncovered to reveal a softened, dark-brown mass of cooked roots with a taste nearly as sweet as molasses.

Since the men were famished, they ate heartily, which led to considerable gastric distress later. Clark wrote, "I find myself verry unwell all the evening from eateing the fish & roots too freely." The next day his troubles continued: "I am verry Sick to day and puke which relive me."

Lewis had been following about eight miles behind Clark and was extremely relieved when Clark sent back a substantial quantity of dried fish and roots, which the party consumed enthusiastically. Refreshed by their brief repast, they caught up to Clark that evening when he "cautioned them of the Consequences of eateing too much." Too late. Lewis and most of the other men became sick within a day or so. Clark observed, "All complain of a Lax & heaviness at the Stomack." Lewis's journal falls silent, but Clark continues to report that many men were "verry sick" and "nearly all Complaining of ther bowels."

This continued for more than a week and did not appear to improve until they managed to kill two deer. But they were back at the roots again by October 6, when Clark wrote, "Capt Lewis & myself eate a Supper of roots boiled, which Swelled us in Such a manner that we were Scercely able to breath for Several hours. . . . Capt Lewis not So well to day as yesterday."

The problem with camas roots as a food source can be explained with simple food chemistry. The main carbohydrate in camas roots (and in several plants in the sunflower family, such as Jerusalem artichoke) is inulin. Balsamroot, another staple food of Northwest Indians, is also rich in inulin. Just as starch is a polymer of glucose, inulin is a polymer of fructose. The breaking down of starch into simple glucose is accomplished through the action of amylases, a common digestive enzyme in humans. Saliva, for instance, is a rich source of amylase. But humans lack the necessary enzymes to break down inulin. Consequently, inulin passes straight through our stomachs and into the intestines, where it encounters a diverse range of bacteria that are fully equipped with the requisite digestive enzymes to deal with inulin, fermenting it into gases such as methane and hydrogen. This process (let's call it flatulogenesis) is similar to what happens with the more famous case of beans, although in that case the recalcitrant carbohydrate is a sugar called raffinose rather than inulin.

In moderation, inulin is reputed to have health benefits related to maintaining a population of desirable intestinal bacteria. For this reason, nearly pure inulin is sometimes sold in health food stores, especially in Europe. But, as the Corps of Discovery discovered, the consequences of an inulin-rich diet can be explosively debilitating, especially if there is a rapid switch from other foods.

Although this topic is not the most pressing issue in modern medical science, there are nevertheless some interesting studies that verify the benefits of inulin in the diet. Studies with cultured bacteria from the intestines show that inulin exerts a stimulatory effect on health-promoting bacteria of the genus *Bifidobacterium* while stifling populations of potentially pathogenic bacteria such as *Escherichia coli* and *Clostridium perfringens* (fig. 3.3).[8] *Bifidobacterium* utilizes inulin

8. See X. Wang and G. R. Gibson, "Effects of the In-vitro Fermentation of Oligofructose and Inulin by Bacteria Growing in the Human Large Intestine."

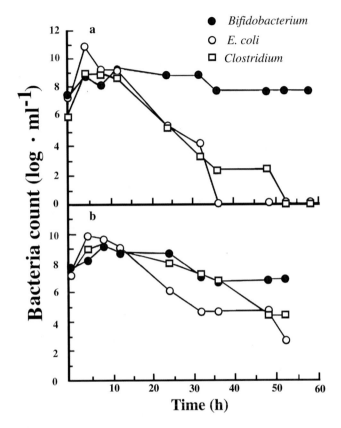

Fig. 3.3. Growth of various intestinal bacteria in culture media with either inulin (A) or glucose (B) as the sole growth substrate. From Wang and Gibson, "Effects of In-vitro Fermentation," 378.

readily and prefers it to other potential food molecules, such as glucose. The same principle applies to the more familiar example of using dairy products supplemented with *Lactobacillus*, another genus of beneficial intestinal bacteria. As in most things in life, moderation is the key.

One of the ways of moderating the effects of inulin is to properly treat the food before ingestion. Pit cooking, as described by Clark,

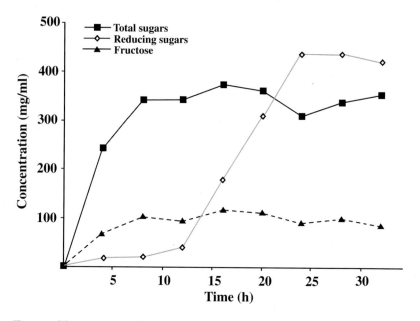

Fig. 3.4. Time course of inulin breakdown in roasting agave rosettes. From Macilli-Margalli and López, "Generation of Maillard Compounds." Reprinted with permission. Copyright 2002 American Chemical Society.

is an effective means of rendering camas and other inulin-rich foods more digestible. Given enough time at the proper heat, the inulin will break down into simpler ("reducing") sugars. For obvious reasons, inulin has never really caught on as a major food in the same way as starch, but, nevertheless, there are cases in which inulin is encountered. One such case is the use of agave, a large, spiny succulent plant from the deserts of Mexico and the southwestern United States. Although the young buds of agave can be eaten, a far more common practice is to use the tough rosettes to make tequila (or mezcal), the national drink of Mexico. The production of tequila requires that the agave be roasted in order to break down the abundant inulin (fig. 3.4). The roasting also results in a carmelization process that produces a host of other chemicals known as Maillard compounds that contribute to the rich and distinctive flavor of tequila (fig. 3.5). These compounds include pyrans and furans for sweet "notes" and aldehydes for "green and floral notes."[9] Although the exact compounds produced by roasting of camas bulbs have not been defined, it is likely that these compounds include Maillard compounds similar to those in agave. Indeed, modern evidence, based on DNA sequence analysis, indicates that Camassia has strong phylogenetic affinities to the agave family (Agavaceae) and is more properly placed in that family than in the lily family (Liliaceae), where traditional morphology-based taxonomy has placed it.[10]

Lewis eventually learned of another way to reduce the bloating caused by camas roots, which he commented on during his return east along the lower Clearwater River in Idaho. On May 16, 1806, he wrote,

> Sahcargarmeah geathered a quantity of the roots of a speceis of fennel which we found very agreeable food, the flavor of this root is not unlike annis seed, and they dispell the wind which the roots called Cows [cous or biscuitroot] and quawmash [camas] are apt to create particularly the latter. we also boil a small onion which we find in great abundance, with other roots and find them also an antidote to the effects of the others. the mush of roots we find adds much to the comfort of our diet.

9. N. A. Mancilla-Margalli and M. G. López, "Generation of Maillard Compounds from Inulin during the Thermal Processing of *Agave tequiana* Weber var. *azul.*"

10. See Martin Pfosser and Franz Speta, "Phylogenetics of Hyacinthaceae Based on Plastid DNA Sequences."

Fig. 3.5. A. Agave "cones" in a crushing pit in Oaxaca, Mexico. After crushing, the pulp will be baked to break down the inulin and then fermented to produce mezcal. B. A still used to produce the final product, which is 40–55 percent alcohol. The square tank at left contains a copper coil submersed in a bath of cool water to condense the alcohol. Photos by author.

There is some uncertainty about the identity of the fennel mentioned by Lewis. It was probably western sweet cicely (*Osmorhiza occidentalis*) or Gairdner's yampah (*Perideridia montana*). The onion was Geyer's onion (*Allium geyeri*), which is common in the area.[11] It is not clear why the captains did not use these plants the preceding spring when they were having such severe intestinal problems.

In fairness to camas, it should be mentioned that at least part of the intestinal problems of the Corps of Discovery can be ascribed to the salmon. The rich flesh of salmon can be a powerful laxative, especially when consumed in excess. This problem was well known to early traders of the Hudson's Bay Company, who often subsisted almostly entirely on dried salmon. The remarks of Thomas Dears, a clerk at a remote outpost on the Thompson River, are typical: "This horrid dried Salmon we are obliged to live upon . . . is quite Medicinal this very morning one of my men in attending the calls of nature evacuated to the distance of six feet."[12] When coupled with the gas-producing potential of camas, the consequences must indeed have been devastating.

The Expedition also collected death camas (*Anticlea elegans* or *Zigadenus elegans*) on July 7, 1806, along the Blackfoot River in western Montana (fig. 3.6). As the name indicates, this is not something you want to eat. All parts of the plant contain the poisonous alkaloid zygadenine, which some claim to be more potent than strychnine. The flowers of death camas would never be confused for true camas, but the leaves and bulbs might. The species often can be found growing together, so collecting the bulbs at times of the year when flowers are absent is risky. Although the captains did bring back a specimen

11. A. Scott Earle and James L. Reveal, *Lewis and Clark's Green World: The Expedition and Its Plants*, 116, 229, 70.

12. James R. Gibson, *Farming the Frontier: The Agricultural Opening of the Oregon Country, 1786 to 1846*, 25.

Fig. 3.6. Death camas (*Anticlea elegans*). Copyright 2007 Mark Turner.

Fig. 3.7. Bitterbrush (*Purshia tridentata*). Photos by Keith Karoly.

of death camas, it is not mentioned in any of the journals. There are no indications that they were ever tempted by death camas or that they knew the specific risks, but they certainly realized the potential hazards of eating unknown plants and wisely relied on advice from the local Indians on numerous occasions.

Purshia tridentata (Bitterbrush)

Bitterbrush was collected by Lewis in Nevada Valley, Powell County, Montana, on July 6, 1806, and received only cursory mention in his journal (fig. 3.7). These specimens still survive with Pursh's annotation, taken from Lewis's notes, that reads: "A Shrub common to the open prarie of the knobs. Jul. 6th 1806."

Pursh placed this plant into the existing African genus *Tigarea,* but it was reassigned to a new genus to honor Pursh (*Purshia*) only three years later by the French botanist Pierre Antoine Poiret when it was realized that bitterbrush is not closely related to *Tigarea.* The specific epithet *tridentata* refers to the three-toothed leaves, a feature (and name) that is shared with big sagebrush (*Artemisia tridentata*). Bitterbrush and big sagebrush are frequently found growing together.

Bitterbrush often grows in great numbers along with sagebrush, or as an understory plant in ponderosa pine forests. It was encountered in abundance by the Expedition. With respect to nutritional content, it is one of the most desirable shrubs for wildlife and is much preferred by them over other shrubs such as sagebrush or rabbitbrush. Cattle are also fond of it, though horses usually avoid it. Overbrowsed bitterbrush has a distinctive appearance in which young branches are heavily trimmed back, leaving stout, gnarled old branches. For the experienced eye it is easy to estimate the size of local deer herds by examining the extent of gnarliness and of survival of young seedlings of bitterbrush. Range managers go to great lengths to enhance bitterbrush numbers and health. They may employ giant vacuum cleaners to harvest seed and elaborate means of overcoming the natural dormancy of seeds before respreading the seed over large areas. The benefits for wildlife and for livestock can be enormous.

Although mule deer were widespread in the pre-European days of the American West, they were not particularly abundant except following localized, periodic disturbances. Lewis and Clark certainly had their share of troubles finding deer or any other game as they made their way through the mountains of central Idaho. But deer numbers increased dramatically following settlement by Euro-Americans. There are several reasons for this increase in deer numbers, but certainly at the top of most lists is the restructuring of plant communities away from dense forests to more open stands with a richer supply of plants suitable for deer browsing, such as bitterbrush. A particularly good example of such changes can be found in the Pitt River Valley in California that was once so empty of deer that early travelers often had to eat their horses or starve.[13] This area is now famous for a large and healthy mule deer population, as well as dense stands of bitterbrush. Similar examples abound elsewhere throughout the West. Humans do indeed find this bush bitter due to a high tannin content and traces of hydrocyanic acid, common in many plants in the rose family (Rosaceae), but it is irresistible candy for deer. No other single wild plant has done as much as bitterbrush to fuel the expansion of deer numbers in the American West.

Bitterbrush seeds are rather large and heavy. They are about the size of a small pea, but more dense. These seeds are not going anywhere without some help, which usually comes in the form of various small rodents. In the ponderosa pine forests of eastern Oregon and Idaho, the chief benefactor is the golden-mantled ground squirrel (*Spermophilus saturatus*), but elsewhere pocket mice, deer mice, kangaroo rats, pack rats, and chipmunks do the job (fig. 3.8).

Fig. 3.8. Golden-mantled ground squirrel (*Spermophilus saturatus*), a common rodent that is responsible for much seed dispersal of bitterbrush. Copyright 2007 Mark Turner.

13. James A. Young and Charlie D. Clements, Purshia: *The Wild and Bitter Roses.*

These rodents are in the habit of carrying seeds around in cheek pouches until they have accumulated a sizable horde, at which time they bury the seeds a few inches deep in the soil. In some areas, practically all regeneration of new bitterbrush seedlings is from seed caches that have been forgotten or abandoned by rodents (fig. 3.9).

As is often the case with temperate, woody plants, bitterbrush seeds display an inherent dormancy that ensures they do not germinate until conditions are proper. In nature, these conditions are met when the seeds are exposed to damp, cool conditions over the winter. However, range managers trying to jump-start bitterbrush stands do not like to rely on this method, since it is slow and subject to the vagaries of weather. Consequently, a great deal of energy has gone into developing artificial means of overcoming this dormancy. Scientists can place their seeds in coolers with trays of wet sand, or they can douse the seeds with various chemicals that leach out or inactivate the dormancy-causing chemicals in the seeds. One popular treatment involves soaking the seeds in a bucket of hydrogen peroxide for five hours. The seeds are then rinsed and dried before eventually being planted out on the range.

Bitterbrush has another feature that may contribute to its success, as well as its high nutrient content. It is one of only a handful of plants outside of the legume family that can fix atmospheric nitrogen. The legume family (Fabaceae—peas, beans, alfalfa, and so on) is distinguished in this regard, since practically all species in this family can fix nitrogen. Through the cooperation of a bacterial partner living in the roots, these plants can take nitrogen gas from the air and convert it into a usable form (ammonia) and then eventually into protein. The bacteria form small swollen structures called nodules on the roots where the nitrogen fixation occurs (fig. 3.10). These plants essentially provide their own fertilizer, whereas other plants have to rely on other forms of nitrogen in the soil, which are usually present in scant amounts. Neither Lewis and Clark nor anyone else at the time had any clue about nitrogen fixation, but the party did manage to collect a few other examples of nonlegumes so endowed:

Fig. 3.9. Young seedlings of *Purshia tridentata* (bitterbrush) emerging in a clump from an old seed cache abandoned by a ground squirrel. Photo by author.

Fig. 3.10. Nitrogen-fixing root nodules on *Purshia*. Photo by author.

Fig. 3.11. Aerial view of an even-aged forest in western Washington. The entire area burned in the late 1920s and was replanted with Douglas-fir. The green stripe (*arrows*) consists of Douglas-fir trees that were interplanted with nitrogen-fixing red alder trees. The alder trees have since died off, but they left behind abundant nitrogen in the soil that has allowed the Douglas-fir trees to be taller and greener than the adjacent trees. Photo courtesy of U.S. Forest Service, Gifford Pinchot National Forest.

three species of alder (*Alnus*), two species of ceanothus or snowbrush (*Ceanothus*), and buffalo berry (*Shepherdia argentea*, which Pursh called *Hippophae argentea*). These plants are particularly successful in areas with low-quality soil or that have been disturbed recently (fig. 3.11). Nitrogen-fixing plants are often responsible for gradually increasing the nitrogen content of the soil to the benefit of subsequent plant communities.

Lomatium (Biscuitroot and Desert Parsleys)

Lomatium is a large genus with more than forty species in the Pacific Northwest alone. Lewis and Clark collected specimens from five species. Several of these plants were staple food items for the Indians, as described in Patrick Gass's journal of April 15, 1806: "The morning was fair. The Commanding Officers attempted to purchase some horses, but could not agree with the Indians on the price; so we proceeded on about four miles to another village, at the mouth of Catarack [today's Klickitat River in Klickitat County, Washington] river. Here we got some Shap-e-leel [*Lomatium*] a kind of bread the natives make of roots, and bake in the sun; and which is strong and palatable."

The species referred to above was probably either *L. cuspidatum* or *L. grayi*.[14] It may have been palatable but likely had a strong aniselike scent and flavor that can be overpowering. Some of the other species of *Lomatium*, especially *L. cous* (cous or biscuitroot), are much more desirable (fig. 3.12). Lewis collected *L. cous* on the north bank of the Walla Walla River in Walla Walla County, Washington, on April 29, 1806, and described it in his journal the next day: "This plain as usual is covered with arromatic shrubs hurbatious plants and a short

14. See Earle and Reveal, *Lewis and Clark's Green World*, for a discussion.

Fig. 3.12. *Lomatium cous* from the Columbia Plateau, Oregon.
Copyright 2007 Mark Turner.

grass. many of those plants produce those esculent roots which form a principal part of the subsistence of the natives. among others there is one which produces a root somewhat like the sweet pittaitoe."

The captains provided more detailed information on cous a few weeks later while the Expedition was marking time at Camp Chopunnish along the Clearwater River in Idaho as they waited for the mountain passes to open. On May 21, 1806, Lewis wrote:

> Today we divided the remnant of our store of merchandize among our party with a view that each should purchase therewith a parsel of roots and bread from the natives as his stores for the rocky mountains. . . . [W]e would make the men collect these roots themselves but there are several speceis of hemlock which are so much like the cows that it is difficult to discriminate them from the cows and we are affraid that they might poison themselves.

Clark followed up on May 28, 1806, with:

> The *Cows* is a knobbed root of an erregularly rounded form not unlike the Gensang in form and Consistence; this root they Collect, rub off a thin black rhind which Covers it and pounding it exposes it in cakes to the Sun. these Cakes are about an inch and 1/4 thick and 6 by 18 in wedth, when dry they either eat this bread alone without any further preperation, or boil it and make a thick Musilage; the latter is most common & much the most agreeable. the flower of this root is not very unlike the gensang—. this root they Collect as early as the Snow disappears in the Spring, and Continues to collect it untill the Quawmash Supplies it's place which happins about the Middle of June. the quawmash is also Collected for a fiew weeks after it first makes it's appearance in the Spring, but when the scape appears it is no longer fit for use untill the Seed are ripe which happens about the time just mentioned. and then the *Cows* declines. The

Cows is also frequently dried in the Sun and pounded after-
wards and used in thickening Supe and Makeing Mush.

Pursh's notes on the herbarium sheet read: "An umbelliferous plant
of the root of which the Wallowallows make a kind of bread. The
natives call'd it Shappalell."

There is little description in the journals as to the culinary qualities of cous, but the Expedition certainly made frequent use of it, as
did the natives. Cous, along with camas, was a main staple for the
Indians of the Columbia Plateau, including the Indians of the Warm
Springs Confederation in central Oregon who still gather and use
the roots each spring. The roots were used in many ways. Whole
roots were sun dried and stored for later use. The roots could also be
pulverized, moistened, partially baked, and mixed in water to make
a passable soup with a parsniplike flavor.

Cous is easier to digest than camas since it contains starch rather
than inulin. At least there are no accounts of Lewis and Clark becoming sick, as they did from camas. A good digger could gather
fifty to seventy-five pounds of biscuitroot in a single day. A pound
of fresh biscuitroot contains 577 Calories, which is high for a wild
food. Compare this to steelhead trout, which possesses 885 Calories
per pound.[15] It is easy to see how a substantial percentage of the
Indians' annual dietary needs could be met by biscuitroot. Although
many species of *Lomatium* were used medicinally by the Indians to
treat infections, apparently cous was not.

Lewis's earlier cautionary note expressing his concern about confusing hemlock with cous is based on some solid field savvy. The
"hemlock" of concern is water hemlock (*Cicuta douglasii*). Unfortunately, the name "hemlock" is also used for a common coniferous tree

15. Alan G. Marshall, "Nez Perce Social Groups: An Ecological Interpretation."

(whose genus is *Tsuga*), which is not toxic and about as closely related to water hemlock as a carrot is to a pine tree. The name "hemlock" can be traced back to the Anglo-Saxon words *hem* (border or shore) and *leác* (leek or plant), hence a leek that is hemmed in. Water hemlock contains cicutoxin, a highly unsaturated alcohol ($C_{17}H_{22}O_2$) that is one of the most dangerous plant toxins known.

A related plant, poison hemlock (*Conium maculatum*), contains the coniine, of fame as the source of Socrates' demise. Coniine is an alkaloid, as are caffeine, nicotine, and morphine. As a class of compounds, alkaloids can have profound effects on most animals, including humans. Even today, poison hemlock is the leading botanical cause of accidental fatal poisoning in humans and a leading killer of livestock.[16] Unlike most other toxic plants, it takes only a small amount (a single bite will do) to be fatal. Death may occur within fifteen minutes, which is probably just as well, since there is no antidote for the toxins. Water hemlock, poison hemlock, and cous are all in the parsley or carrot family (Apiaceae) and do look enough alike that there is the potential for confusion, though probably not more than once. If Lewis had been more experienced with the local flora, he would have realized that cous is a dryland plant, whereas water hemlock is found only on wet soils beside or in streams, but his decision not to depend on his men to tell the difference was certainly prudent.

Mahonia (Oregon Grape)

Lewis and Clark were the first to characterize what we now know as Oregon grape. This decorative shrub is very common as

---

16. See E. P. Krenzelok and F. J. Provost, "The 10 Most Common Plant Exposures Reported to Poison Information Centers in the United States."

an understory plant in forests of the Pacific Northwest and elsewhere in the West. It features leaves that look like holly and edible
berries that look like blueberries. It is used extensively in landscap-
ing. One species (*M. aquifolium*) is distinguished as the state flower
of Oregon (fig. 3.13). When Pursh first examined samples of this
plant, he thought it was unique enough to be a new genus and briefly
considered naming it *Lewisia*. After more deliberation, however, he
decided it should be placed in an existing genus, *Berberis,* which
is how it appeared in his book *Flora Americae Septentrionalis.* The
name *Mahonia* was given later by Thomas Nuttall, a naturalist who
traveled extensively in the western United States. The genus was
named after Bernard McMahon, the noted gardener and seedsman
who was so important in organizing the botanical foundation of the
Lewis and Clark Expedition, as mentioned earlier. Both *Mahonia*
and *Berberis* are names used by modern botanists today depending
on whether one is a "lumper" who wishes to include Oregon grape
in the much more widespread genus of *Berberis* or a "splitter" who
thinks the presence of compound leaves is distinction enough to rate
a separate genus. Most modern taxonomists, at least those in the
United States, prefer assigning these plants to *Berberis,* but even so
the name *Mahonia* is still valid as a section name, a sort of subgenus
to which these plants belong. Furthermore, mahonia is sometimes
used as a common name. Finally, the official residence of the governor of Oregon is called Mahonia Hall, which does seem to bear the
weight of governmental authority.

The explorers encountered three species of *Mahonia: M. aquifolium*
(shining or tall Oregon grape), *M. nervosa* (Cascade or dull Oregon
grape), and *M. repens* (creeping Oregon grape). The first encounter,
with *M. repens,* was recorded by Gass on September 1, 1805, as the
group passed through present-day Lemhi County in Idaho: "There
is also a small bush grows in this part of the country, about 6 inches

Fig. 3.13. Oregon grape (*Mahonia* [or *Berberis*] *aquifolium*).
Photo by Keith Karoly.

high, which bears a bunch of small purple berries. Some call it mountain holly; the fruit is of an acid taste."

The other two species were described by Lewis with his typical attention to botanical detail on February 12, 1806, as the explorers were waiting out the sodden weather at Fort Clatsop on the Oregon coast:

> There are two species of ever green shrubs which I first met with at the grand rappids of the Columbia and which I have since found in this neighbourhood also; they grow in rich dry ground not far usually from some watercourse. the roots of both species are creeping and celindric. the stem of the Ist [*M. aquifolium*] is from a foot to 18 inches high and as large as a goosqu[i]ll; it is simple unbranc[h]ed and erect. it's leaves are cauline, compound and spreading. the leafets are jointed and oppositely pinnate, 3 pare & terminating in one, sessile, widest at the base and tapering to an accuminated point, an inch and a quarter the greatest width, and 3 inches & a 1/4 in length. each point of their crenate margins armed with a subulate thorn or spine and are from 13 to 17 in number. they are also veined, glossey, carinated and wrinkled; their points obliquely pointing towards the extremity of the common footstalk. . . . The stem of the 2nd [*M. nervosa*] is procumbent abo[u]t the size of the former [*M. aquifolium*], jointed and unbranched. it's leaves are cauline, compound and oppositely pinnate; the rib from 14 to 16 inches long celindric and smooth. . . . I do not know the fruit or flower of either. the Ist resembles the plant common to many parts of the U'States called the mountain holley.

As was often the case, Clark copied Lewis's journal nearly word for word so that there would be a backup copy in case one journal should be lost or damaged. Clark went a step further and provided sketches of the leaves of both species.

As mentioned by Gass, the berries are edible, though not particularly choice. Even today, hard-core westerners like to make jam from Oregon grape, but this has more to do with civic pride and pioneer spirit than it does with gustatory excellence. However, if you put enough sugar in it, it does taste sort of sweet. Some people will even mix in berries from salal (*Gaultheria shallon*), another common native shrub with bland fruit that was also collected by Lewis and Clark.

Xerophyllum tenax (Bear-grass)

Bear-grass is common and widespread in the Pacific Northwest. Its tall (two to three feet), showy floral heads and large tufts of basal, linear leaves are very conspicuous and easy to identify even from a distance (fig. 3.14). Despite its name and appearance, it is not a grass at all. It is placed in either the lily family (Liliaceae) or the obscure bunch-flower family (Melanthiaceae), depending on which botanist you ask. The genus name is derived from the Greek *xeros* (dry) and *phyllon* (leaf) in reference to the tough, wiry leaves. Two specimens survive in the herbarium sheets from the Expedition, both dated June 15, 1806, when the captains were passing through present-day Lolo County and Idaho County, Idaho. Lewis provided commentary a few days later, on June 26: "There is a great abundance of a speceis of bear-grass which grows on every part of these mountains it's growth is luxouriant and continues green all winter but the horses will not eat it."

Pursh's notes on the herbarium sheets make reference to the fact that the Indians used the leaves of this plant extensively to make "baskets & other ornaments." The captains had numerous occasions to observe this practice and often mentioned it briefly in their journals. The most detailed example comes from January 17, 1806, during the sodden winter at Fort Clatsop, when Lewis noted:

Fig. 3.14. Bear-grass (*Xerophyllum tenax*) from the Cascade Range, Oregon. Copyright 2007 Mark Turner.

Their baskets are formed of cedar bark and beargrass so closely interwoven with the fingers that they are watertight without the aid of gum or rosin; some of these are highly ornament-ed with strans of beargrass which they dye of several colours and interweave in a great variety of figures; this serves them the double perpose of holding their water or wearing on their heads; and are of different capacites from that of the smallest cup to five or six gallons.

Bear-grass is not a species that has attracted much attention from scientists, but it is such a common sight in parts of the West that it is worth remembering Lewis and Clark's role in its discovery.

CHAPTER 4

Cottonwood

T he Expedition encountered a wide range of vegetation types as they traversed the West—from open, treeless plains to massive coniferous rain forests with some of the world's tallest trees. Despite this great diversity, one type of tree was a constant companion practically the whole way. Seldom were they out of sight of at least one species of cottonwood. Sometimes they remarked on the presence of as many as three different types of cottonwood at one site. Cottonwoods are trees of the riverbanks. Since Lewis and Clark were river travelers, it is not surprising that cottonwoods were constantly at hand. The journals contain literally hundreds of entries relating to cottonwood. Paul Cutright says of cottonwood, "Of all western trees it contributed to the success of the Expedition more than any other."[1]

The cottonwoods of North America can be found in a variety of species and subspecies. Black cottonwood (*Populus trichocarpa,*

---

1. Cutright, *Lewis and Clark,* 232.

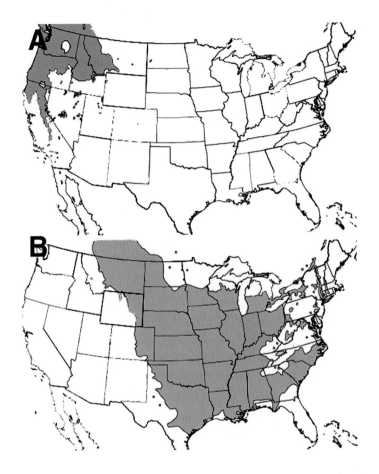

Fig. 4.1. Distribution of (A) black cottonwood (*Populus trichocarpa*) and (B) eastern cottonwood (*Populus deltoides*). From U.S. Department of the Interior, U.S. Geological Survey, "Digital Representation of 'Atlas of United States Trees' by Elbert L. Little, Jr.," n.p.

fig. 4.1A) is the largest hardwood tree in the West, reaching heights of up to 150 feet, with trunk diameters in excess of 5 feet. Black cottonwood is extremely common along the Columbia River and its tributaries. Eastern cottonwood (*Populus deltoides,* fig. 4.1B) is arguably the largest tree of any type in the East. The national record holder, which is in Seward, Nebraska, has a diameter of almost 12 feet.[2] The taxonomy of this species is messy, with several subspecies being generally recognized, including the Great Plains cottonwood (*P. deltoides* subsp. *monilifera*). The men of the Expedition were no doubt very familiar with cottonwoods from the East.

Lewis unwittingly became ensnared in the complicated taxonomy of cottonwoods on June 12, 1805, while in present-day Chouteau County, Montana, when he described a species of cottonwood previously unknown to science: narrow-leafed cottonwood (*Populus angustifolia*):

> The narrow leafed cottonwood grows here in common with the other species of the same tree with a broad leaf or that which has constituted the major part of the timber of the Missouri from it's junction with the Mississippi to this place. The narrow leafed cottonwood differs only from the other in the shape of it's leaf and greater thickness of it's bark. the leaf is a long oval acutely pointed, about 2 1/2 or 3 Inches long and from 3/4 to an inch in width; it is thick, sometimes slightly grooved or channeled; margin slightly serrate; the upper disk of a common green while the under disk is of a whiteish green; the leaf is smoth. the beaver appear to be extremely fond of this tree and even seem to scelect it from among the other species of Cottonwood, probably from it's affording a deeper and softer bark than the other species.

It is likely that Lewis collected this tree, but the specimen was lost along with many other samples when the cache that they left while westbound near the Great Falls of the Missouri was destroyed

---

2. American Forests, "National Register of Big Trees," n.p.

by flooding. The plan was to retrieve the specimens on the return trip east. This loss was extremely discouraging to Lewis, since all the specimens collected by Lewis between the Mandan villages and Great Falls on the trip west were also lost. At any rate, the detail evident in Lewis's description is ample evidence of his botanical prowess.

Cottonwoods often form sheltering groves along riverbanks and thus offered good shelter for camp. There are many references in the journals to camps located near cottonwood stands. Wildlife also found shelter in cottonwood trees, a fact that did not escape the attention of hunters during the Expedition. Cottonwoods can survive in the arid West in large part because they have deep roots that tap into groundwater. Consequently, the trees can be used as distant sentinels that signal the presence of water to parched travelers. They also served as visual beacons that guided Expedition members back to the river.

Cottonwood was especially important as the Expedition crossed the Great Plains, because it was practically the only tree of any size. Certainly, cottonwood was indispensable during the winter of 1804–1805 at Fort Mandan when it was the main source of firewood. The wood burned quickly, especially when dried driftwood was used. At one stretch in January, Lewis recorded the following temperatures (°F) at sunrise on thirteen consecutive days: -18, -4, -14, -28, -20, -11, -22, -20, -21, -40, -38, -20, -34. At such times, a warm fire was critical to their survival. Dried buffalo chips might work fine to cook a summer meal on a campfire, but for keeping warm at -40, you need something a bit more substantial.

Cottonwood was the wood of choice (and often necessity) for construction. The Indians also used cottonwood trees as poles to form the frame for tepees. Lewis on July 13, 1805, noted one extraordinarily large such lodge that "was formed of sixteen large cottonwood poles each about 50 feet long and at their larger end which rested on the ground as thick as a man's body. [The lodge] was 216 feet in circumpherence at the base. . . . [I]t was probably designed for some great feast, or a council house on some national concern."

Taking their cue from the Indians, the Expedition primarily used cottonwood logs, some up to eighteen inches in diameter, to construct Fort Mandan for their first winter in the field. They also built a goodly amount of furniture from cottonwood, including tables, beds, benches, and other miscellaneous items for use around camp. Although cottonwood is soft, it does split well. It would not be the choice for fine furniture to last for years, but it was easy to work, functional, and, most important, available.

The Expedition fashioned some twenty-two-inch-diameter wagon wheels out of cottonwood while portaging the Great Falls of the Missouri. Lewis was not particularly happy with that situation, since the wood was "extremely illy calculated for it being soft and brittle" but still found it fortunate because he did "not believe we could find another of the same size perfectly sound within 20 miles of us." His judgment proved right, as he later complained of the frequent repairs that were necessary to keep the wagons working.

On several occasions it was necessary to fashion canoes from cottonwood. For instance, before they left Fort Mandan, the men fashioned six dugouts from cottonwood trees found a few miles above the fort. These canoes were somewhat awkward on the water, but they were adequate for the job. The next summer, Clark would construct more dugouts while exploring the Yellowstone River. The cottonwood logs he used were twenty-eight feet long, sixteen to eighteen inches deep, and sixteen to twenty-four inches wide. These were a bit small for the purpose, so he lashed them together side by side to increase stability. The softness of the wood was now a convenience that made constructing the canoes easier than it otherwise would have been. In any case, there were no other trees available that were large enough.

While at Fort Mandan, Lewis reported that the Indians fed the inner bark of cottonwood to their horses in winter, a practice apparently previously unknown to Euro-Americans and especially important out on the plains, where winter feed was scarce. The practice was still common on the northern plains eighty years later, when Theodore Roosevelt observed, "Often, in winter, the Indians cut down the cottonwood trees and feed the tops to their ponies; but this is not done to keep them from starving, but only to keep them from wandering off in search of grass. Besides, the ponies are very fond of the bark of the young cottonwood shoots, and it is healthy for them."[3]

As usual, the Indians were astute naturalists in their use of cottonwood bark. Later studies have shown that the inner bark of cottonwood is about threefold richer in protein during the fall and winter than the summer.[4] Once new growth begins in the spring, this protein is utilized in the growing leaves. The differences in protein can be clearly visualized using a technique called SDS-PAGE (sodium dodecyl sulfate polyacrylamide gel electrophoresis). In short, this technique involves grinding up the leaves to make a protein soup and then separating the proteins in a gelatinous slab through which an electric current is passed. Once properly stained, the proteins appear as tiny bands corresponding to proteins of different sizes. As can be seen clearly in figure 4.2, there is much more protein in cottonwood bark in the winter months.

The seasonal differences in protein content can also be seen clearly with a microscope (fig. 4.3). In this case, cells from the winter bark are packed with small vesicles consisting of protein. By summer,

3. Roosevelt, *Ranch Life and the Hunting-Trail.*

4. See S. C. Wetzel, C. Demmers, and J. S. Greenwood, "Seasonally Fluctuating Bark Proteins Are a Potential Form of Nitrogen Storage in 3 Temperate Hardwoods."

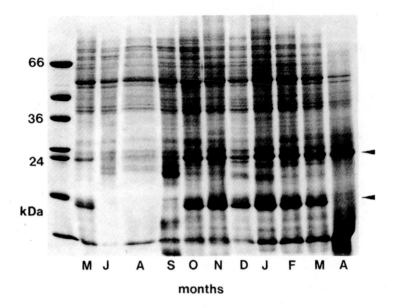

Fig. 4.2. Separation of protein in extracts from cottonwood bark. Bands correspond to individual proteins. Each vertical lane corresponds to the month indicated beneath. Note the especially intense bands during the winter months, as indicated by the arrows at right. The column on the far left contains molecular-weight standards of sizes (kiloDaltons), as indicated. From Wetzel, Demmers, and Greenwood, "Seasonally Fluctuating Bark Proteins." Copyright 2004 Springer.

those same cells appear mostly empty, with their insides taken up by a large watery vacuole with little protein.

Cottonwoods and other poplars remain today as icons of the West. Quaking aspen (*Populus tremuloides*) stands as a symbol of untrammeled beauty in the mountains, especially when garbed with its golden-yellow fall foliage. The exotic Lombardy poplar (*Populus nigra* var. *italica*) is perhaps the most commonly planted tree of the open plains and Intermountain West, where its tall columnar shape and

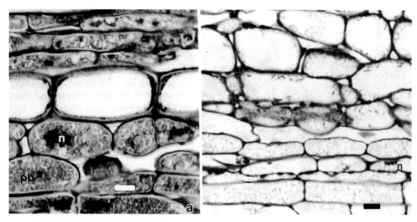

Fig. 4.3. Microscopic view of cottonwood bark from (A) winter and (B) summer: *n*, nucleus; *pb*, protein bodies; bars = 10 μm. From Wetzel, Demmers, and Greenwood, "Seasonally Fluctuating Bark Proteins."

fast growth are handy for providing shade and windbreak, especially around ranch homes. Lombardy poplar is a peculiar tree. Despite its abundance in the West, it is not native, and it cannot reproduce sexually. Like most trees in the willow family, poplars are dioecious, that is, the male and female flowers are on separate individuals. All Lombardy poplars are males. Lombardy poplar arose as the result of a bud sport (mutation in one bud) in a tree in Italy sometime in the early 1700s. Every individual of Lombardy poplar is a direct descendant of that individual bud. Since there are no females, no seeds can be produced. All propagation is by shoot cutting or by sprouting from the roots.

Poplars have another big asset going for them. They grow rapidly. This has not escaped the attention of foresters. In addition, the trees are very easy to clone, propagate, and manipulate genetically, both by traditional breeding and by genetic engineering. Hybrids between eastern cottonwood and black cottonwood capture the large-girth capabilities of the former with the exceptional height of the latter, resulting in a tree with exceptional vigor and value. The wood is soft but is ideal for making paper or for processing into strand (flake) board.

Hybrid poplars can reach a height of sixty feet in as little as six years and produce between four and ten dry tons of wood per acre per year, up to four times the yield for managed pine plantations (fig. 4.4).[5] Yields of this magnitude require intensive management, including the application of fertilizers, insecticides, and (especially in the West) irrigation water. There are already more than one hundred thousand acres of hybrid poplars cultivated in the Pacific North-west (including British Columbia), with the total increasing rapidly. These are not natural forests, but, on the other hand, the harvest of hybrid poplars can be viewed as an alternative to the destruction of natural forests, and thus there can be considerable environmen-tal advantages. Where would you rather have your newspaper come from, old-growth stands in a national forest or managed fields of hybrid poplar grown on private land?

There are other potential environmental gains to be had from hybrid poplars. All that biomass could be turned into ethanol to fuel automobiles. Brazil does that with sugarcane. In fact, about half of the automobile fuel in Brazil comes from ethanol produced from sugarcane. We could probably do the same in the United States with poplar after investing in the development of appropriate tech-nology. The ethanol would contain almost no sulfur to contribute to air pollution. Furthermore, the CO_2 released would not contribute to rising levels of CO_2 in the atmosphere because it would just be returning CO_2 to the air where the trees got it in the first place. Although it would require a lot of land, the scale is not prohibitive, nor is the technology. Just using the idle farmland that the federal

5. See Oak Ridge National Laboratory, "Popular Poplars," n.p.

Fig. 4.4. Harvesting of a seven-year-old hybrid poplar growing in western Oregon along the Columbia River. Photo by Steve Strauss.

government pays farmers to set aside would go a long way toward meeting the need. The real barriers are mostly political and economical.

As great as hybrid poplars are, it might be possible to make them even better. Poplars are ideal targets for genetic engineering, being much more amenable to these manipulations than most other tree species. Without going into a detailed debate on the merits or perils of genetic engineering, suffice it to say that it is my opinion as a professional botanist and ardent environmentalist that it makes a lot of sense to genetically engineer poplars. The potential upside for environmental benefits is massive. Although some ecopurists will hedge at genetic engineering, it is shortsighted to argue against something that will (1) reduce logging in our public forests, (2) reduce consumption of fossil fuels, (3) reduce use of harsh agricultural chemicals, and (4) reduce use of dioxin-producing bleaches for paper manufacturing.

Here is how it could work: Hybrid poplars are grown as a farm crop—large fields of monoculture, just like corn, except the rotation period is six years rather than six months. Weeds and insects can be a problem. Currently, they are managed with the use of chemicals, some of which are not exactly what you want to seep into your groundwater. As has been done with soybean, corn, cotton, and many other crops, it is now a fairly straightforward enterprise to create poplars that produce their own insecticide or that are resistant to fairly benign herbicides such as glyphosate (as in the product Roundup).[6] The insect resistance is provided by a gene from a bacterium (*Bacillus thuringiensis,* or Bt) that allows for the production of a toxic protein that kills caterpillars. Organic gardeners have been using the Bt protein for years, although not from genetically engineered sources.

6. See Kees van Frankenhuyzen and Tannis Beardmore, "Current Status and Environmental Impact of Transgenic Forest Trees."

Suddenly, it becomes possible to maintain healthy poplars without the application of harsh insecticides.

Work is also under way to develop poplar lines that produce wood with a reduced lignin content. The wood produced by these trees can be more easily processed into paper with significantly less use of environmentally harmful chemicals such as chlorine bleach, notorious as a source of dioxin. Aspen trees (a close relative of cottonwood)

Fig. 4.5. Enhanced growth in transgenic ten-week-old aspen plants. The control plant on the left is "wild type" (that is, a natural line), whereas the four plants to the right have all been altered genetically to produce less lignin. From Hu et al., "Repression of Lignin Bio-synthesis," 810. Reprinted by permission of Macmillan Publishers Ltd. Copyright 1999 Nature America, Inc.

that have been engineered to produce less lignin can actually channel more resources into cellulose production and thus produce not only "cleaner" wood but also about 15 percent more of it (fig. 4.5).[7]

The concept of genetic engineering of this type raises concerns, partially of a philosophical nature, that are beyond the scope of this book. Especially troublesome is the vision of the escape of foreign genes into native trees and the subsequent corruption of natural forests. Most scientists are convinced that the risks can easily be managed with careful science. For instance, it will be necessary (and straightforward) to develop sterile hybrids to avoid the unintentional spread of foreign genes to native cottonwoods. There is some comfort in the fact that millions of mutant Lombardy poplars have already been planted in the West and there has been no problem with rogue genes spreading to other poplars. Surprisingly, Lombardy poplars have been widely planted in the United States for such a long time that even Lewis was familiar with them, which he described as "that beatifull and celibrated tree the Lombardy poplar."[8] Assuming the environmental concerns can be fully addressed, the main barrier to widespread use of transgenic poplars will be public misconceptions.

7. See Wen-Jing Hu et al., "Repression of Lignin Biosynthesis Promotes Cellulose Accumulation and Growth in Transgenic Trees."

8. Moulton, "Journals . . . Botanical Collections," http://www.lewisandclark journals.unl.edu, codex R, p. 4.

CHAPTER 5

Rain Forests

The winter of 1805–1806 provided an opportunity for Lewis to concentrate on his role as a naturalist. Freed from the rigors of daily travel and route planning, he finally had the time to focus on the plants and animals around him. The coast of western Oregon and Washington consists of a temperate rain forest with huge, exotic trees and an overwhelming dripping mossiness that must have seemed otherworldly to woodsmen from eastern forests. The mild climate, secure housing, and abundant food in the form of elk also contributed to his "leisure time," or at least time that was not occupied with the necessities of survival. During this winter, Lewis discovered and described ten plants, eleven birds, two fish, and eleven mammals that were new to science.[1] He also provided detailed observations on hundreds of other species that were only slightly known from elsewhere.

1. Cutright, *Lewis and Clark*, 273.

The forests surrounding Fort Clatsop were representative of the greatest temperate rain forests in the world. These forests have basic properties that are very different from the eastern deciduous forests that the men of the Expedition knew so well. The trees were huge, perhaps pushing four hundred feet tall, easily twice the height of the tallest trees in the East. These trees were not just tall. They were massive as well, with trunks thirty feet or more in circumference. Evergreen conifers dominated the biomass by a factor of one thousand, again vastly different from most eastern forests. The evergreen lifestyle is particularly well suited to this climate, since it allows for photosynthesis to continue throughout much of the cool and wet part of the year (November through April). Deciduous trees are at a disadvantage, because their activity is restricted to the summers, which are typically dry in the Pacific Northwest.

Lewis turned his attention to the giant conifers in early February after life at Fort Clatsop had settled into a routine. His detailed account of the Sitka spruce (*Picea sitchensis*) from February 4 is typical and goes a long way toward disproving his opening disclaimer that his botanical skills were "slender":

> There are sveral species of fir in this neighbourhood which I shall discribe as well as my slender botanicall skil will enable me and for the convenience of comparison with each other shal number them. (No 1). a species which grows to immence size; very commonly 27 feet in the girth six feet above the surface of the earth, and in several instances we have found them as much as 36 feet in the girth or 12 feet diameter perfectly solid and entire. they frequently rise to the hight of 230 feet, and one hundred and twenty or 30 of that hight without a limb. this timber is white and soft throughout the rives better than any other species which we have tryed. the bark skales off in irregula rounded flakes and is of a redish brown colour particularly of the younger growth. the stem of this tree is simple

branching, ascending, not very defuse, and proliferous. the leaf of this tree is acerose, 1/10th of an Inh in width, and 3/4 of an Inch in length; is firm, stif and accuminate; they are triangular, a little declining, thickly scattered on all sides of the bough, but rispect the three uppersides only and are also sessile growing from little triangular pedestals of soft spungy elastic bark. at the junction of the boughs, the bud-scales continue to incircle their rispective twigs for several yeas; at least three years is common and I have counted as many as the growth of four years beyond these scales. this tree affords but little rosin. it's cone I have not yet had an opportunity to discover altho' I have sought it frequently; the trees of this kind which we have felled have had no cones on them.

Over the next two days, Lewis devoted considerable journal space to similar descriptions of other conifers, including grand fir (*Abies grandis*), Douglas-fir (*Pseudotsuga menziesii*), western hemlock (*Tsuga heterophylla*), and western white pine (*Pinus monticola*). Lewis was also impressed with western hemlock, which he described as being "next in dignity in point of size. it is much the most common species, it may be sa[i]d to constitute at least one half of the timber in this neighbourhood. it appears to be of the spruse kind."

He was mistaken in thinking it was a spruce, but the taxonomy of conifers was somewhat lax at the time. Clark was even more lax, since he generally referred to any evergreen conifer as a "pine." Both spruce and hemlock are evergreen conifers in the pine family (Pinaceae), so the captains were not too far off the mark. No doubt they recognized the strong resemblance of this species to Canadian hemlock (*Tsuga canadensis*) that is common in the eastern United States. Throughout his writings, Lewis made frequent comparisons to plants of the eastern United States with which he was familiar. His description of western white pine was typical in this regard: "the white pine; or what is usually so called in Virginia. I see no difference between this and

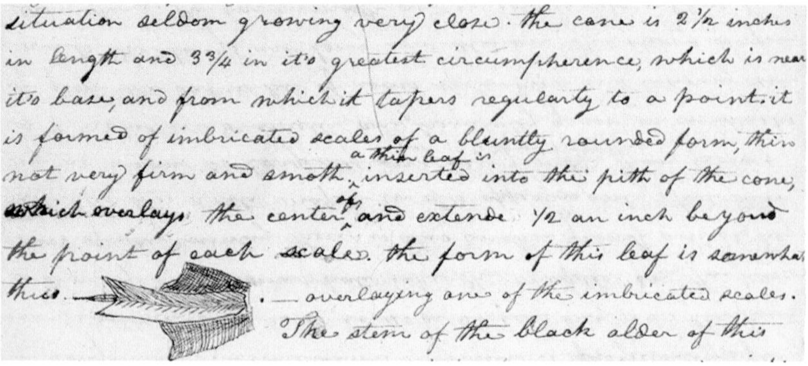

situation seldom growing very close. the cone is 2 1/2 inches in length and 3 3/4 in it's greatest circumpherence, which is near it's base, and from which it tapers regularly to a point. it is formed of imbricated scales of a bluntly rounded form, thin not very firm and smoth, a thin leaf is inserted into the pith of the cone, which overlays the center of and extends 1/2 an inch beyond the point of each scales. the form of this leaf is somewhat thus. — overlaying one of the imbricated scales. The stem of the black alder of this

Fig. 5.1. Sketch of a portion of the cone of Douglas-fir from Lewis's journal of February 9, 1806 (codex J, p. 65). The "thin leaf" he refers to is technically a subtending bract. Copyright American Philosophical Society.

that of the mountains in Virginia; unless it be the uncommon length of cone of this found here, which are sometimes 16 or 18 inches in length and about 4 inches in circumpherence. I do not recollect those of virginia perfectly but it strikes me that they are not so long." As usual, Lewis's skills as a naturalist were right on the mark. Eastern white pine (*Pinus strobus*) is common in the mountains of Virginia and is indeed almost identical to western white pine except for the larger cone size of the latter (fig. 5.1).

Of all the conifers of the West Coast, western red-cedar (*Thuja plicata*) was clearly the most important for the Indians. This one species provided food, shelter, clothing, hats, baskets, weapons, ropes, medicine, transportation, and even diapers. Indeed, the East Coast cousin of this tree (*Thuja occidentalis*) bears the common name arborvitae, literally "tree of life," a name that dates back to the sixteenth century, when the French explorer Jacques Cartier learned from the Indians along the St. Lawrence River how to use the tree's foliage to treat scurvy. The tree's health-bestowing benefits arise from the high content of vitamin C (ascorbic acid) in the foliage. Lewis was famil-

INSIDE OF AN INDIAN LODGE.

Fig. 5.2. The inside of an early Indian lodge from the coast of the Pacific Northwest. The timbers are primarily red-cedar. Salmon are hanging from the rafters to dry. Oregon Historical Society, no. 58496.

Fig. 5.3. An early, undated photograph of a typical Indian dugout canoe along the Columbia River. Oregon Historical Society, no. 36828.

iar with the East Coast version and called western red-cedar "arbor vita or white cedar" on numerous occasions in the journals.

The wood of western red-cedar is a marvel of natural engineering. Light yet strong, it is extremely resistant to rot, making it the ideal choice for construction of structures and canoes (figs. 5.2 and 5.3). Its wood is surprisingly tough, yet soft enough to be worked by simple tools. The Expedition encountered numerous impressive cedar lodges while on the lower Columbia River, such as the one Lewis described on April 6, 1806:

> It consisted of seven appartments in one range above ground each about 30 feet square. the entrances to these appartments were from passages which extended quite across the house, about 4 feet wide and formed like the walls of the hose of broad boards set on end extending from beneath the floor to the roof of the house. the apperture or hole through which they enter all those wooden houses are remarkably small not generally more than 3 feet high and about 22 inches wide this house is covered with the bark of the white cedar, laid on in a double course, supported by rafters and longitudinal round poles attatched to the rafters with cores of this bark. the peices of the cedar bark extend the whole length of the side of the roof and jut over at the eve about 18 inches. at the distance of 18 inches transverse splinters of dry fir is inserted through the cedar bark in order to keep it smooth and prevent it's edges from colapsing by the heat of the sun; in this manner the natives make a very secure light and lasting roof of this bark. in the vicinity of this house Capt. Clark observed the remains of five other large houses.

The timbers used for these lodges were usually of western red-cedar— a prudent choice, since timber from any other tree species would rot quickly due to the wet climate and semisubterranean nature of these structures.

While at Fort Clatsop on January 15, 1806, Lewis took note of how the local Indians used cedar to construct their bows:

> Their bows are extreamly neat and very elastic, they are about two and a half feet in length, and two inches in width in the center, thence tapering graduly to the extremities where they are half an inch wide they are very flat and thin, formed of the heart of the arbor vita or white cedar, the back of the bow being thickly covered with sinews of the Elk laid on with a gleue which they make from the sturgeon; the string is made of sinues of the Elk also.[2]

The bark of western red-cedar is fibrous and thus provides a convenient material from which to make cordage for a variety of uses. The fibers could be used to weave simple articles of clothing or sandals. Conical hats, important for shedding the constant rain of the coastal climate, were also constructed from cedar bark. In addition, the inner bark of cedar is edible. The captains did not remark on this, but fortunately Sergeant Gass was sufficiently curious about this practice to record the following in his journal on April 5, 1806, as they passed near Sandy River in Oregon: "The soil is rich with white cedar timber, which is very much stripped of its bark, the natives making use of it both for food and clothing."

Lewis's attitude toward these incredibly gigantic trees sounds almost passively clinical to today's ears. These trees were of a scale unimaginable by East Coast or European standards (figs. 5.4 and 5.5). Perhaps his senses had become saturated by the fantastic sights he had encountered almost daily since leaving St. Louis. But he was

---

2. Local Indians also constructed bows out of Pacific yew (*Taxus brevifolia*), which would probably have been a better choice for reasons of strength. Medieval English longbows were made from the English yew (*Taxus baccata*).

Fig. 5.4. A large Sitka spruce along the Oregon coast (Lincoln County) in 1923. Oregon Historical Society, no. 57563.

Fig. 5.5. An extremely large (fifty-seven-foot circumference) western red-cedar from Arlington County in western Washington. The notch cut into the face is to receive a "springboard" upon which the chopper can stand to avoid having to cut through the swollen butt of the tree. Oregon Historical Society, no. 81516.

Table 5.1. Properties of common evergreen conifers in the Pacific Northwest encountered by Lewis and Clark

Species	Typical age (years)	Maximum age (years)	Typical diameter (feet)	Maximum diameter (feet)
Douglas-fir (*Pseudotsuga menziesii*)	>750	1,200	5.6–8.2	16.1
Sitka spruce (*Picea sitchensis*)	>500	>750	6.7–8.6	19.5
Western red-cedar (*Thuja plicata*)	>1,000	>1,200	5.6–11.2	23.5
Western hemlock (*Tsuga heterophylla*)	>400	>500	3.4–4.5	23.5
Western white pine (*Pinus monticola*)	>400	615	4.1	7.3
True fir[a] several species (*Abies* spp.)	>400	>500	3.3–5.6	10.0
Ponderosa pine (*Pinus ponderosa*)	>600	726	2.8–4.7	9.9
Western larch[b] (*Larix occidentalis*)	>700	915	5.2	8.7

Sources: Compiled from Richard H. Waring and Jerry F. Franklin, "Evergreen Coniferous Forests of the Pacific Northwest"; Robert Van Pel, *Forest Giants of the Pacific Coast*; and American Forests, "National Register of Big Trees."

Maximum height (feet)	Remarks from Lewis and Clark journals
393–413 (historical records)	"The bark thin, dark brown, much divided with small longitudinal interstices and sometimes scaleing off in thin rolling flakes. . . . [T]he wood is redish white 2/3ds wn the center, the ballance white, somewhat porus and tough" (February 6, 1806).
205	"In several instances we have found them as much as 36 feet in the girth or 12 feet diameter perfectly solid and entire" (February 4, 1806).
195	"The women have a kind of fringe petticoats, made of filaments or tassels of the white cedar bark wrought with a string at the upper part, which tied round the waist" (November 17, 1805). "Some of these Indians Wore hats which they make out of white Cedar & bear Grass" (November 19, 1805).
241	"It is much the most common species, it may be sa[i]d to constitute at least one half of the timber in this neighbourhood [Fort Clatsop]. . . . [I]t rises to the hight of 160 to 180 feet very commonly and is from 4 to 6 feet in diameter, very stright round and regularly tapering" (February 5, 1806).
227	"This Species is not common I have Seen it only in three instances since I have been in this neighbourhood [Fort Clatsop]" (February 6, 1806). "The arrow is formed . . . of light white pine reather larger than a swan's quill, in the lower extremity of this is a circular mortice secured by sinues roled arround it" (January 15, 1806).
278	"This tree affords considerable quantities of a fine clear arromatic balsam in appearance and taste like the Canadian balsam" (February 6, 1806).
227	"The Indians have pealed a number of Pine for the under bark which they eate at certain Season of the year" (September 12, 1805). "The seed of this speceis of pine is about the size and much the shape of the seed of the large sunflower; they are nutricious and not unpleasant when roasted or boiled" (May 8, 1806). "The long leafed pine forms the principal timber of the neighbourhood [Missoula County, Montana], and grows as well in the river bottoms as on the hills" (July 2, 1806).
189	"The country through which we passed is extreemly fertile and generally free of stone, is well timbered with several speceis of fir, long leafed pine and larch" [well known in the East] (June 10, 1806).

aIncludes silver fir (*A. amabilis*), grand fir (*A. grandis*), and noble fir (*A. procera*). Douglas-fir is not a true fir.

bLarch is a conifer but not evergreen. It is deciduous.

clearly impressed by one particularly large Sitka spruce his men encountered on March 10, 1806:

> The hunters who were over the Netull [Lewis and Clark River]
> the other day informed us that they measured a pine tree, (or fir
> No 1) [Sitka spruce] which at the hight of a man's breast was
> 42 feet in the girth about three feet higher, or as high as a tall
> man could reach, it was 40 feet in the girth which was about the
> circumpherence for at least 200 feet without a limb, and that it
> was very lofty above the commencement of the limbs. from the
> appearance of other trees of this speceis of fir and their account
> of this tree, I think it may be safely estimated at 300 feet. it had
> every appearance of being perfectly sound.

These trees that Lewis was describing—specifically Sitka spruce
and Douglas-fir—are among the largest species of trees in the world,
and Lewis was fortunate to encounter them in their prime (table
5.1). The oldest were one thousand years old. Although it is true
that the coastal redwood (*Sequoia sempervirens*) of California is the
current record holder for height (379 feet),[3] Douglas-fir is a close
second and may actually have had taller individual trees in the past.
One Douglas-fir is reliably reputed to have been 413 feet tall.[4]

Almost all of the truly big trees are now gone. Sitka spruce was
an early victim. It grows exclusively along the coast, rarely more than
twenty miles inland, and thus was easily accessible and transportable.
As if to double-seal its fate, navies from around the world have vigor-
ously sought Sitka spruce for centuries because its size and strength
make it by far the best type of wood from which to construct masts

3. Richard Preston, "Tall for Its Age," 36. The three tallest trees in the world, all
redwoods, were discovered in just 2006.

4. Al Carder, *Forest Giants of the World, Past and Present.*

for sailing ships. Douglas-fir has a much wider distribution and remains today as the most important commercial timber tree in the Pacific Northwest. But the really huge trees such as those described by Lewis and Clark are mostly gone, with the exception of those preserved in national and state parks. Even counting these reserves, less than 8 percent of original old growth remains.

Fortunately, there are a few big trees left. There are at least 116 individual redwood trees more than 350 feet tall, all in northern California.[5] Douglas-fir has not fared as well, since fewer of the really big ones escaped logging. None of the big trees that Lewis and Clark saw around Fort Clatsop remain. The first permanent settlement on the Pacific coast (Astoria, named after John Jacob Astor's Pacific Fur Company) was established nearby only five years after Lewis and Clark left, and the loggers followed soon thereafter. The location at the mouth of Columbia allowed for easy transport of timber. In fact, there are only a few small pockets of old-growth trees left anywhere along the Oregon coast. Nowadays, if you want to see prime coastal old growth, your best bet is to go to the Olympic National Park in northern Washington.

The states of Oregon and Washington have a long-standing battle to claim the record Douglas-fir. The current Oregon record is held by a giant tree in the Coos Bay area that tops out at 329 feet, but slightly taller trees were found in Washington in 1998.[6] Determining champion trees is somewhat subjective, since it is customary to consider other factors besides height, such as the diameter at breast height, volume, and crown spread. Often, the trees with really large diameters have tops that are broken out so that it becomes a matter of speculation as to what the actual or potential height could have been.

5. George W. Koch et al., "The Limits to Tree Height."
6. Van Pelt, *Forest Giants*.

Since the criteria vary, it is difficult to declare a true title holder for "world's biggest tree," and various foresters have their favorite candidate, usually depending on what corner of the world their patch of woods is in. Even Australia can make a credible claim with the giant mountain-ash (*Eucalyptus regnans*), which historical records suggest may have reached well over 400 feet, but such claims are highly speculative, since ALL of the really tall mountain-ash trees are gone.

What are the driving evolutionary forces that lead to such massive scale in these trees? The obvious answer is, of course, the quest for light that all plants need for photosynthesis. The story of light has some unique slants (literally) in the temperate rain forests of the Pacific Northwest. This part of the world has what is known as a Mediterranean climate—dry summers and wet but mild winters. Lewis and Clark got their fill of this damp, dreary climate during their winter on the Oregon coast. For instance, in December 1805, it rained every day at Fort Clatsop, all 31 days. The weather report from December 28 was typical: "rained as usial, a great part of the last night, and this morning rained and the wind blew hard from the S. E."

One can also sense their despair. And then—relief on January 1: "sun visible for a few minutes about 11 A.M." before the rain returned. During their 137 days at Fort Clatsop, the Corps of Discovery experienced some form of precipitation (almost always rain) on 121 days.[7] The temperature was so mild that Lewis wrote on January 14, 1806: "weather perfectly temperate. I never experienced a winter so warm as the present has been."

This climate favors evergreen trees such as Douglas-fir, hemlock, and Sitka spruce. Since they retain their leaves in the wet, mild winters, they can continue to photosynthesize. Douglas-fir manages

7. Paul A. Knapp, "Window of Opportunity: The Climatic Conditions of the Lewis and Clark Expedition of 1804–1806."

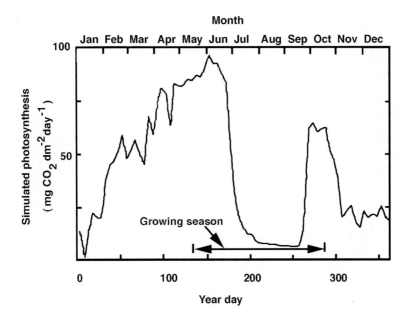

Fig. 5.6. Seasonal pattern of photosynthesis by Douglas-fir in the Pacific Northwest. Note that much of the yearly total of photosynthesis occurs outside the normal growing (frost-free) season. From Waring and Franklin, "Evergreen Coniferous Forests," 1383. Reprinted with permission. Copyright 1979 American Association for the Advancement of Science.

to complete about 40 percent of its total annual photosynthesis during the off-season when deciduous hardwoods like maples and oaks have no leaves (fig. 5.6). Obviously, this gives evergreens a considerable advantage. Here is where the slant on light becomes important. Since these forests are fairly far north (Fort Clatsop is about 46° N latitude), the angle of the sun is low in the winter. In order to intercept as much light as possible, the trees need to be tall and lean, as opposed to broad and spreading (fig. 5.7). So the incentive is not just to be tall to reach the light, but to have an elongated geometry that maximizes the interception of low-angle light. This tall, lean

Fig. 5.7. Aerial view of a typical old-growth forest in the Cascades Mountains of Washington. Photo by the author.

approach also helps to slough off snow that would be much more problematic with long branches and a spreading crown. Spreading crowns work great in a tropical rain forest, but tall and lean is the way to go in a temperate rain forest.

What determines the limit of tree height? If 300 feet is good, is 400 feet better? Or 500 feet? This is a valid scientific question that has yielded some interesting answers lately. It is not, as you might imagine, simply a matter of engineering, although that can be a factor. Wood is surprisingly strong as well as flexible, and the general consensus is that structural integrity is not the ultimate limiting factor, at least in sheltered valleys where strong winds are rarely encountered. Despite its deserved reputation for stormy weather, the Pacific Northwest virtually never encounters hurricanes or tornadoes.

Tall trees have a real problem getting enough water to their tops, and this is most likely the factor that limits their theoretical height.

A needle at 300 feet off the ground is a long way removed from the roots. Trees, being vascular plants, move water through conductive tissue called xylem—better known simply as wood. It is one of the more seldom-appreciated botanical wonders that this movement is accomplished over great distances (300 feet or more) against the force of gravity with absolutely no energy being spent by the plant. A large Douglas-fir may move hundreds of gallons each day to its upper foliage, but it does not spend a single calorie doing so. The driving force is provided by evaporation from the leaves (more properly called transpiration), which in turn sucks the water up from below through the xylem. It really is a sucking force, a true suction, and the water in the xylem is under a negative pressure. The degree of suction is substantial, often exceeding twenty times normal atmospheric pressure. The higher off the ground, the greater is the sucking force required to raise the water up. It takes about one extra atmosphere of suction for each 30 feet that the water is raised.[8] A leaf sitting 300 feet in the air can be really stressed by such forces. If the leaf cannot pull up enough water, it becomes drier and drier, pulling harder and harder with the foliar equivalent of pursed lips, until the leaf either stops growing or dies. Either way, that tree is not going to get any taller.

There is a new breed of adventurous tree physiologists who have lent support to this explanation by climbing or being hoisted into the world's tallest trees and measuring photosynthesis and leaf moisture (fig. 5.8).[9] As expected, there is a distinct gradient as one moves higher in the canopy. Photosynthesis declines with height according to a set mathematical relationship. By extrapolating this relationship to heights exceeding the actual tree height, it is possible to predict at what height photosynthesis would be zero. Even though there are

8. More precisely, about -0.01 MegaPascals per meter.
9. Koch et al., "Limits to Tree Height," 851.

Fig. 5.8. The Wind River Canopy Crane Research Facility, operated by the U.S. Forest Service and the University of Washington, allows researchers easy access to the tops of tall trees in an old-growth forest in western Washington. The scientist at right is measuring photosynthesis in fir needles 180 feet above the forest floor. Courtesy of the Wind River Canopy Crane Research Facility Image Archives.

no existing trees taller than 379 feet, the formula predicts a theoretical maximum height of 410 feet, a number in close agreement with creditable historical records for the tallest trees. Furthermore, other mathematical relationships (for example, moisture versus height and carbon isotope versus height) can also be extrapolated to provide similar estimates, all falling in the range of 410 to 430 feet.

Lewis's description of the massive trees around Fort Clatsop was accurate for the most part but strangely lacking in passion. How can a dedicated naturalist and woodsman such as Lewis not get excited when he discovers some of the largest trees in the world? Part of the answer may lie in the fact that he wished to remain a clinical observer whose purpose was to make an accurate record without emotional embellishment. However, it is also likely that Lewis was influenced by the general attitude of his time in which humans, especially early Americans, viewed nature as either an adversary to be feared or conquered or a limitless resource. Even Jefferson, who was a great advocate of nature in the New World and a tremendous influence on Lewis, held his highest regard not for wildlands but for tranquil countrysides with a pastoral or agricultural flavor.[10] This worldview was recorded eloquently by the famous French aristocrat Alexis de Tocqueville during his travels in America in 1831–1832:

> In Europe people talk a great deal of the wilds of America, but the Americans themselves never think of them till they fall beneath the hatchet. They are insensible to the wonders of inanimate nature and they may be said not to perceive the mighty forests that surround them till they fall beneath the hatchet. Their eyes are fixed upon another sight . . . the . . . march across these wilds, draining swamps, turning the courses of rivers, peopling solitudes, and subduing nature.[11]

It is harsh to condemn Lewis as insensitive, since he was a product of his time, as are we all. Besides, the journals are full of instances in which Lewis clearly was in awe of the natural beauty around him. But, in 1806, America had plenty of trees, so a few more, even big ones, did not send Lewis into fits of ecstasy. There would be time later for the John Muirs, Henry David Thoreaus, and Aldo Leopolds to awaken the American spirit.

10. See Roderick Nash, *Wilderness and the American Mind.*
11. Tocqueville, *Democracy in America*, 148.

CHAPTER 6

Salmon

R oughly speaking, the Indians of the American West relied primarily on two animals for food. The Plains Indians ate mostly buffalo, and their culture revolved around that magnificent animal. The Indians west of the Rockies ate mostly salmon, and their culture correspondingly was centered on fish to the extreme. For reasons that are not entirely clear, there were no buffalo west of the Rocky Mountains. But there were prodigious numbers of salmon. Although the numbers fluctuated from year to year, the total run in the Columbia River system alone in pre-Euro-American times was probably ten to sixteen million fish per year.[1]

The waters of the Pacific Northwest are blessed with five species of salmon (chinook, coho, sockeye, chum, and pink), as well as two species of anadromous (sea-running) trout (steelhead and cutthroat) with similar life histories (figs. 6.1–6.3). All seven species are so closely related that they are usually included in the genus *Oncorhynchus*

---

1. James A. Lichatowich, *Salmon without Rivers,* 180.

Fig. 6.1. Adult chinook salmon making a spawning run in the Elwha River in Washington State. Copyright Natalie Fobes.

Fig. 6.2. Adult sockeye salmon in a lake on the Alaska Peninsula. Copyright Natalie Fobes.

Fig. 6.3. Coho salmon eggs and recently hatched aelvins in a hatchery on the Sol Duc River in Washington State. Copyright Natalie Fobes.

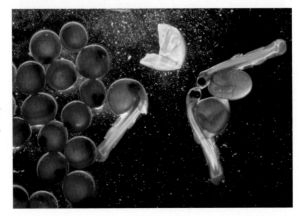

Table 6.1. Salmonids of the Expedition

Journal name	Modern name	Scientific name
Common salmon	Chinook or king salmon	*Oncorhynchus tshawytscha*
Red charr	Sockeye salmon	*Oncorhynchus nerka*
White salmon trout	Coho or silver salmon	*Oncorhynchus kisutch*
Salmon-trout	Steelhead	*Oncorhynchus mykiss*
Mountain or speckled trout	cutthroat trout	*Oncorhynchus clarkii*

Note: It is likely that the Expedition also encountered chum salmon (*Oncorhynchus keta*) and pink salmon (*O. gorbuscha*), but the journals are not clear about this.

Remarks from the journals
"It is this speceis that extends itself into all the rivers and little creeks on this side of the Continent, and to which the natives are so much indebted for their subsistence. the body of this fish is from 2 1/2 to 3 feet long and proportionably broad. it is covered with imbricated scales of a moderate size and is variagated with irregular black spots on it's sides and gills. . . . [T]he roes of this fish are much esteemed by the natives who dry them in the sun and preserve them for a great length of time. they are about the size of a small pea nearly transparent and of a redish yellow colour" (Lewis, March 13, 1806).
"The red Charr are reather broader in proportion to their length than the common salmon, the skales are also imbricated but reather large. the nostrum exceeds the lower jaw more and the teeth are neither as large nor so numerous as those of the salmon. some of them are almost entirely red on the belly and sides; others are much more white than the salmon and none of them are variagated with the dark spots which make the body of the other. their flesh roes and every other particular with rispect to their form is that of the Salmon" (Lewis, March 13, 1806).
"The prime back fin and ventral ones, contain each ten rays; those of the gills thirteen, that of the tail twelve, and the small fin placed near the tail above has no bony rays, but is a tough flexable substance covered with smooth skin" (Lewis, March 16, 1806).
"Seldom more than two feet in length, they are narrow in purportion to their length, at least much more So than the Salmon & red charr. their jaws are nearly of the Same length, and are furnished with a Single Series of Subulate Streight teeth, not so long or so large as those of the Salmon, the mouth is wide, and the tongue is also furnished with Some teeth. the fins are placed much like those of the Salmon. at the Great Falls are met with this fish of a Silvery white colour on the belly and Sides, and a blueish light brown on the back and head" (Clark, March 13, 1806).
"These trout are from sixteen to twenty three inches in length, precisely resemble our mountain or speckled trout[a] in form and the position of their fins, but the specks on these are of a deep black instead of the red or goald colour of those common to the U.'States. these are furnished long sharp teeth on the pallet and tongue and have generally a small dash of red on each side behind the front ventral fins; the flesh is of a pale yellowish red, or when in good order, of a rose red"[b] (Lewis, June 13, 1805).

[a]According to Moulton, Lewis is referring to the brook trout, *Salvelinus fontinalis*, a common species in the eastern United States (*Journals of the Expedition*, 4:288).

[b]This is the first informal description of this subspecies for Western science.

(table 6.1). The cutthroat trout (*O. clarkii*) was technically described in 1836 by Sir John Richardson who named it in honor of William Clark. This species claims the prize for the most thoroughly Lewis-and-Clark-ized of all due to two recognized subspecies: *O. clarkii lewisi* (from Montana) and *O. clarkii clarki* (from British Columbia).

The Expedition saw their first salmon on August 13, 1805, shortly after crossing the Continental Divide. Lewis wrote: "An indian called me in to his bower and gave me a small morsel of the flesh of an antelope boiled, and a peice of a fresh salmon roasted; both which I eat with a very good relish. this was the first salmon I had seen and perfectly convinced me that we were on the waters of the Pacific Ocean."

From that point on the Expedition encountered salmon, in one form or another, practically every day until they crossed back over the Rockies the following summer. The Indians were extremely proficient at harvesting salmon, and eager to exchange the fish for goods offered by the captains. Weirs were a popular method for salmon capture, as described a few days later, on August 21, by Lewis:

> This morning early Capt. C. resumed his march; at the distance of five miles he arrived at some brush lodges of the Shoshones inhabited by about seven families here he halted and was very friendly received by these people, who gave himself and party as much boiled salmon as they could eat; they also gave him several dried salmon and a considerable quantity of dried chokecherries. after smoking with them he visited their fish wear which was abut 200 yds. distant. he found the wear extended across four channels of the river which was here divided by three small islands. three of these channels were narrow, and were stoped by means of trees fallen across, supported by which stakes of willow were driven down sufficiently near each other to prevent the salmon from passing. about the center of each a cilindric basket of eighteen or 20 feet in length terminating in a conic

shape at it's lower extremity, formed of willows, was opposed to a small apperture in the wear with it's mouth up stream to receive the fish. the main channel of the water was conducted to this basket, which was so narrow at it's lower extremity that the fish when once in could not turn itself about, and were taken out by untying the small ends of the longitudinal willows, which formed the hull of the basket.

Although Indians were scattered all along the Columbia River and its tributaries, the greatest concentration of people as well as the pinnacle of salmon culture was at Celilo Falls, about eight miles east of present-day The Dalles, Oregon (fig. 6.4). The falls, often described

Fig. 6.4. Indians fishing for salmon at Celilo Falls on the Columbia River in 1945. Note the safety lines that secure fishermen to the shore as they perch on unstable wooden platforms and use large dip nets to scoop out salmon. With permission of the Historic Photo Archive.

as one of the greatest rapids in the world, were swallowed up by im-
pounded water when the gates of The Dalles Dam were closed in
1957. The area was a traditional meeting place and trading site for the
tribes of the Columbia. It also marked the transition point between
the Shahaptian and Chinookan languages. Regrettably, it is now only
a wayside stop along Interstate 84. Clark offered a vivid description
of the scene at Celilo Falls on October 17, 1805:

> The number of dead Salmon on the Shores & floating in the
> river is incredible to Say and at this Season they have only to
> collect the fish Split them open and dry them on their Scaffolds
> on which they have great numbers, how far they have to raft their
> timber they make their Scaffolds of I could not lern; but there
> is no timber of any Sort except Small willow bushes in Sight in
> any direction. . . . Saw great numbers of Dead Salmon on the
> Shores and floating in the water, great numbers of Indians on
> the banks viewing me and 18 canoes accompanied me from the
> point—The Waters of this river is Clear, and a Salmon may be
> Seen at the deabth of 15 or 20 feet. West 4 miles to the lower
> point of a large island near the Stard. Side at 2 Lodges, passed
> three large lodges on the Stard Side near which great number
> of Salmon was drying on Scaffolds one of those Mat lodges I
> entered found it crouded with men women and children and
> near the enterance of those houses I saw maney Squars engaged
> Splitting and drying Salmon. I was furnished with a mat to Sit
> on, and one man Set about prepareing me Something to eate,
> first he brought in a piece of a Drift log of pine and with a
> wedge of the elks horn, and a malet of Stone curioesly Carved
> he Split the log into Small pieces and lay'd it open on the fire
> on which he put round Stones, a woman handed him a basket
> of water and a large Salmon about half Dried, when the Stones
> were hot he put them into the basket of water with the fish
> which was Soon Suficently boiled for use. it was then taken

out put on a platter of rushes neetly made, and Set before me
they boiled a Salmon for each of the men with me, dureing
those preperations, I Smoked with those about me who Chose
to Smoke which was but fiew, this being a custom those people
are but little accustomed to and only Smok thro form. after
eateing the boiled fish which was delicious.

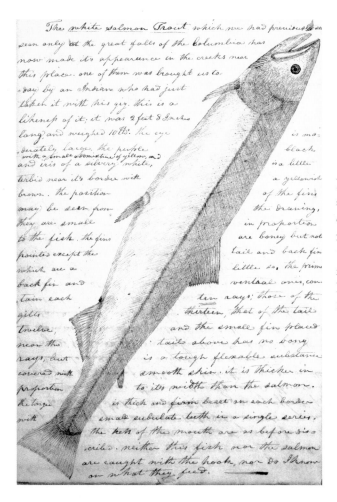

Fig. 6.5. Clark's sketch of a coho salmon from March 16, 1806. Copyright American Philosophical Society.

Clark provided more details on how the Indians used the salmon a few days later, near present-day Wishram, Washington (fig. 6.5):

> I observe great numbers of Stacks of pounded Salmon <butifully> neetly preserved in the following manner, i e after Suffiently Dried it is pounded between two Stones fine, and put into a speces of basket neetly made of grass and rushes of better than two feet long and one foot Diamiter, which basket is lined with the Skin of Salmon Stretched and dried for the purpose, in theis it is pressed down as hard as is possible, when full they Secure the open part with the fish Skins across which they fasten tho' the loops of the basket that part very Securely, and then on a Dry Situation they Set those baskets the Corded part up, their common Custom is to Set 7 as close as they can Stand and 5 on the top of them, and secure them with mats which is raped around them and made fast with cords and Covered also with mats, those 12 baskets of from 90 to 100 w. each <basket> form a Stack. thus preserved those fish may be kept Sound and Sweet Several years, as those people inform me, Great quantities as they inform us are Sold to the whites people who visit the mouth of this river as well as to the nativs below.

Salmon are widely regarded today as one of the most delicious of all fish. Health-conscious people rightly depend on salmon as a main component of their diet and will pay premium prices for fresh wild fish. Salmon are a rich source of omega-3 fatty acids that decrease the risk for heart disease, inflammatory processes, and some types of cancer. Clark certainly developed an appreciation for it, declaring steelhead, fried in bear oil, to be "the finest fish I ever tasted." But the captains' high regard for salmon began to fade after months of a monotonous diet of fish. Often their only variety was in how they got their salmon: dried, boiled, fried, smoked, or pounded into cakes. Lewis in particular developed a strong dislike for salmon, much preferring to eat dogs instead. It takes a lot of dogs to keep thirty hungry, active men (plus Sacagawea) fed, but the Expedition never missed a chance to buy all they could from the Indians, sometimes purchasing as many as forty in one day. As Paul Cutright so eloquently put it, "Until they climbed back over the Continental Divide the following spring, back to the land of beaver tail and buffalo hump, they reduced the dog population of the Columbia River valley appreciably."[2]

Scholars have long been puzzled by the lack of bison in the Intermountain West in pre-Euro-American times. Various theories have been advanced, including the possibility that forage quality was inadequate or snow depths too great. Although these possibilities cannot be dismissed outright, they are not entirely satisfying or convincing. A more plausible explanation may have been provided by Clark, who with his usual powers of observation and deduction wrote on August 29, 1806, "I have observed that in the country between the nations which are at war with each other the greatest numbers of wild animals are to be found." This theory has been developed extensively by Paul S. Martin and Christine R. Szuter who note that the bison-rich lands along the Upper Missouri and Yellowstone Rivers were largely uninhabited by humans except for transitory bands of Indian war parties.[3] The peaceful lands farther west consisted of a "game sink" that had been stripped of most of its large animals by humans. If correct, this is another manifestation of the human-driven extinction of the megafauna as discussed in Chapter 1. It is likely that much larger populations of bison, deer, and other large animals would have flourished in the Intermountain West were it not for heavy human hunting pressure.

2. Cutright, *Lewis and Clark*, 219.
3. See Martin and Szuter, "War Zones and Game Sinks in Lewis and Clark's West."

The dietary constraints of the Expedition raise an interesting question. What did Seaman, Lewis's magnificent Newfoundland dog, eat while in the Pacific Northwest? Was he expected to eat dog meat, as the men did? Or did he eat mostly salmon? A salmon-rich diet is a risky undertaking for a dog because of salmon-poisoning disease, which can be fatal. The disease is caused by a rickettsial organism, *Neorickettsia helminthoeca,* that is carried by a parasitic trematode (flatworm or fluke) in the fish. The disease is particularly prevalent west of the Cascade Range. Neither the microbe nor the fluke is particularly troublesome for the fish, but if a dog eats raw or improperly cooked fish, then the fluke may burst open, releasing the microbe that then kills the dog. Bears, cats, and other mammals (including humans) are not affected. Thorough cooking prevents the disease, but it has to be done properly. Most dogs are avid fans of raw salmon and seldom miss an opportunity to consume any carcasses they might find lying around. Perhaps the Indians warned Lewis to keep a close check on Seaman at all times when around the rivers and to make sure all his salmon was thoroughly cooked. Nowadays, these flukes can be easily seen with the unaided (though trained) eye in the flesh of most wild salmon in the Northwest. Perhaps they were less common in the past and have become more common as the health of western rivers has declined. The mystery of Seaman's diet must remain unsolved, as the journals seldom even mention his name. It is generally assumed that he survived the trip, but even that point is not clear.

Anyone who has spent any time in the modern Pacific Northwest is aware that salmon are a powerful and omnipresent icon for the region. Salmon can still be caught in the Willamette River in downtown Portland, as well as many other rivers and streams of the region. But the numbers of salmon these days are distressingly low compared to the runs seen by Lewis and Clark. In the Columbia basin, the runs are about 1.7 percent of historic levels. The percentage remaining for all of California, Oregon, Washington, and Idaho is only a little better (5.2 percent).[4] Fortunately, the runs in Alaska are as strong as ever. On the other side of the Pacific, along the one thousand–mile-long Kamchatka Peninsula, the same species of salmon (plus two others) are also doing exceedingly well. But that is little consolation for the residents of the lower states who see the demise of salmon as a serious diminishment of the natural wealth of the region and a manifestation of man's misguided attempts to use technology and science to subdue nature.

What happened to the salmon, and can we bring them back? Those questions are the moon shot of modern fish biology. If we throw enough money (billions of dollars) at the problem and turn our best scientists and engineers loose, maybe we can restore wild runs to historic levels. Unfortunately, that is not realistic. The fixes that would be required are so radical that they are not worth contemplating unless Earth First! takes over the federal government. Even though there are no simple answers, we owe it to the fish and to ourselves to do what we can. We cannot expect to restore the salmon to their former glory, but we can and should keep them around in reasonable numbers in the Pacific Northwest. Accomplishing that feat involves a complex blend of science, economics, and politics. Solutions are evasive in part because the science is not clear. There is even a good case to be made for the argument that science (or at least technology) has been part of the problem, not the cure.

Many factors have contributed to the precipitous decline in numbers of salmon. These include river-choking dams, habitat loss due to extensive logging and overgrazing, runoff from mining and road construction, industrial pollution, dredging to facilitate river

---

4. Robert T. Lackey, "Restoring Wild Salmon to the Pacific Northwest: Chasing an Illusion?"; http://www.epa.gov/wed/pages/staff/lackey/pubs/illusion.htm#historical, table 2.

navigation, overfishing, genetic dilution of wild stocks with inferior hatchery-bred or farm-raised ("ranched") fish, and natural cycles of temperature and nutrients in the ocean. If there is to be any progress toward the issue of salmon restoration, then modern biology needs to provide some clear answers. Many minds are at work on just that.

Dams are the most conspicuous player in the salmon-killing equation. It is not easy to overlook a twenty-four-million-ton plug of concrete and steel, such as the Grand Coulee Dam in northern Washington (fig. 6.6). There are eighteen main-stem dams on the Columbia River and its main tributary, the Snake River. Most of the dams have various technological fixes to help the salmon pass through, but not the Grand Coulee. It is 550 feet high and has no fish ladders. Not one single salmon can get past the Grand Coulee to the 1,400 miles of prime salmon habitat that lies above in the

Fig. 6.6. A salmon's eye view of the Grand Coulee Dam on the Columbia River in Washington State. Photo by the U.S. Bureau of Reclamation.

headwaters of the Columbia River in British Columbia. There have been tremendous economic gains from this dam, but it has come at a cost. Similarly, Hells Canyon Dam on the Snake River on the Idaho-Oregon border is 330 feet high and is also an absolute barrier to salmon.

A huge amount of research and engineering expertise has gone into trying to make the other dams more fish friendly. A proper understanding of the life history of salmon is necessary to understand what it takes to make this work. Salmon are anadromous, meaning that they hatch in freshwater rivers where they rear for a year or two. They then migrate to and mature in the ocean. After an additional two to five years in the ocean, they return to their place of origin, displaying an amazing ability to sniff out the exact stream in which they were hatched. For most Pacific salmon, the return trip ends in spawning and then death. (Steelhead and Atlantic salmon may survive to return to the ocean and subsequently spawn again.) Incidentally, Lewis was not aware of this aspect of salmon biology and was puzzled by the large numbers of dead and dying chinook salmon along the Columbia River. As a consequence of this life history, salmon must pass each dam twice during their life—once as a juvenile smolt on the way out to the ocean and a second time as an adult on the way back to spawn. Each passage takes its toll.

The upstream trip as an adult is probably the more renowned, and certainly the more conspicuous, of the two, but it is actually the downstream trip that is most problematic. A lot of thought has gone into fish ladders, and most of them work well for the upstream-bound adults. A high percentage of adults make it past even the main-stem dams (except for Grand Coulee and Hells Canyon dams), thanks to proper engineering of the ladders. But consider for a moment the plight of the juveniles headed downstream for saltwater.

Juveniles (also called smolts) are by nature small and fragile. Their first problem is just figuring out which way is downstream. Now that the dams have turned the rivers into a series of languid reservoirs, there is little flow to sweep the smolts on their way. If they are lucky enough to get to the dam, another problem arises. If that dam is going to be useful, most of the river's flow is going to go through the turbines to make electricity. Those turbines will also make a lot of sushi. Even if a smolt survives the turbine ride, it is going to be spit out into a maelstrom of highly aerated water below the dam. Confused and disoriented, the young fish also suffers from too much nitrogen gas dissolved in the water. The gas results in nitrogen narcosis in which nitrogen bubbles form in its blood. This is the same thing as the "bends" that afflict deep-sea divers if they ascend too rapidly. It can be just as fatal to fish as it is to man. Even if the bends don't get it, our poor Maytagged fish may be temporarily dazed and immobile, making it easy prey for larger predator fish such as northern pikeminnow (*Ptychocheilus oregonensis,* formerly called northern squawfish), which have figured out that just below the dam is a great place to wait for lunch. Assuming the juvenile salmon survives, that is just the first dam, and more await downstream.

With those problems in mind, dam engineers and river managers (mainly the Army Corps of Engineers and Bonneville Power Administration [BPA]) can do a lot to shift the odds in favor of the young salmon. One obvious and fairly inexpensive fix is to install screens over the turbines to keep the young fish out. These screens are effective in diverting about 60–70 percent of spring and summer chinook salmon, but only about 30 percent of fall chinook salmon. Another easy fix is to open the spillways to release more water downriver. The juveniles are carried over the dam and flushed downriver by the increased flow. This works but is very expensive. Spilled water does not generate electricity, and millions of potential dollars are lost. Also, care must be taken that the water is released properly. Just opening a standard spillway is a bad idea because the nitrogen narcosis that results from the agitated water will kill the fish. To mitigate this problem, seven of the eight lower Columbia and Snake dams have been retrofitted with spillway deflectors (also called flip lips) that limit the plunge depth of the water with the result that less nitrogen gas is mixed in with the water. Other experimental and very expensive reengineering projects for spillways are planned over the next few years. Even with these engineering adjustments, some dams simply cannot be made suitable for the safe downstream passage of young salmon. At those dams the Army Corps collects the young salmon on the upstream side of the dams and loads them onto trucks or barges for transportation around the dam.

The federal river managers at the BPA have even come up with a way to reduce the toll that predator fish take on the young salmon. Since 1990, the BPA has been paying a bounty of four to eight dollars per fish on pikeminnow to anyone willing to catch them. A few specially tagged pikeminnow are worth five hundred dollars! Pikeminnow are not normally sought by fishermen because their soft, bony flesh is not good to eat. But the bounty has created a lot of interest, especially from retired fishermen who appreciate the opportunity to congregate just below the dams with their fishing buddies and make a few extra bucks. More than 267,000 pikeminnow were caught in 2004 alone, reducing predation on juvenile salmonids by about 25 percent.[5]

Lewis also knew about the pikeminnow, which he called mullet. He provided science with its first glimpse of this species that he characterized on April 17, 1806, as the Expedition worked its way up the Columbia River near The Dalles, Oregon: "The inhabitants of the rapids at this time take a few of the white salmon trout and considerable quantities of a small indifferent mullet on which they

5. Pacific States Marine Fisheries Commission, "Northern Pikeminnow Sport Reward Fishery," n.p.

principally subsist. I have seen none except dryed fish of the last season in the possession of the people above that place." This brief fragment is the only mention of pikeminnow in the journals. The captains did not consider it noteworthy, and the Indians ate it only when they could not get salmon.

Dams are only part of the salmon's problems. Some people would say the dams are not even the main problem. Overfishing and habitat degradation had already led to substantial declines in salmon runs before the first dam ever went in. The incredible natural abundance of salmon provided opportunities for huge profits once cannery technology caught on. The first cannery on the Columbia River was constructed in 1866, and others followed soon thereafter throughout practically all major rivers in the Pacific Northwest. At first, the supply of fish seemed inexhaustible. Great wealth flowed out of the rivers and into the pockets of a small group of cannery entrepreneurs. But such unregulated exploitation could not be sustained. The cannery yield peaked on the Columbia as early as 1895.[6] By 1915, the cannery packs at all other locations in Washington and Oregon had begun their inevitable decline. The age of the big dams was still more than twenty years away.

Hatcheries are often held up as the salvation of Pacific salmon. This opinion is especially prevalent among river managers, politicians, and old-school fish biologists, but this view is increasingly coming under fire from a new breed of fish scientists. It is certainly true that the vast majority of salmon (about 90 percent) in the Columbia and almost all other rivers in Oregon and Washington these days are hatchery fish. Since wild fish are largely protected from harvest, there would be little sportfishing for salmon without the hatchery fish. (Hatchery fish have clipped fins so that fisherman can

6. Lichatowich, *Salmon without Rivers,* 90.

tell which ones are keepers.) The hatcheries were conceived (mostly by politicians in the 1930s through 1950s) as a compromise solution to the question of whether to build dams. Although the science of salmon biology was astoundingly primitive at the time, it was obvious to the fish biologists even then that the dams would be devastating. The issue was put frankly in a report from the U.S. Fish and Wildlife Service to the Army Corps of Engineers in 1944: "No competent fishery biologist is willing to assert that the salmon runs can be preserved if the full program of construction does go through." They foresaw that fish ladders and other technological fixes would simply be "monuments to a departed race."[7]

But there were strong economic forces at work, and most of the dams went through. The politicians attempted to pacify the public by claiming that it was possible to have both power and fish. Each approval of a new dam was accompanied by the funding of a compensatory hatchery. In theory, the idea had merit, but things have not really worked out the way they were intended.

One of the hard-learned lessons of modern salmon biology is that not all fish are created equal. In the early days, eggs from the Sacramento or Columbia rivers were transferred to hatcheries on other rivers throughout the West. Some even made it to East Coast rivers. Most of these transfers failed spectacularly, because it was not recognized that salmon are highly adapted to their local streams. Eventually, adjustments were made so that egg sources more closely matched the actual streams in which the smolts would be released. (Foresters in the Pacific Northwest learned the same lesson the hard way with respect to the importance of using site-appropriate seed sources when replanting.) Salmon numbers have spurted back here and there but nowhere near historic levels. A more serious concern

7. Ibid., 187.

is the effect that hatchery fish have on the ecosystem and on wild salmon. These are the spiny issues to which much modern research has been directed.

The importance of genetic diversity is a central theme in modern conservation biology. Salmon need to swim in a deep gene pool in order to survive and prosper in nature. Even if hatchery managers try to introduce diversity, there is no way they can match the richness of natural variation. Besides, hatchery fish are wimps. Raised and pampered in near ideal conditions, the young are not put through the discriminating trials of evolutionary selection that wild fish face. The weak or poorly adapted do just fine. This is a diluted, Disney-like view of nature, and one that will inevitably lead to the development of a weakened race. Nature, like business, science, sports, romance, and most other human endeavors, needs competition. The strong must be rewarded. Darwin was not kidding about this.

The disadvantages of hatcheries have been demonstrated in elegant studies pitting hatchery-raised coho against wild coho.[8] The fish in these experiments were kept in a controlled stream channel in which breeding competition and density were carefully manipulated. The hatchery fish proved inferior with respect to many important measurements of fitness. Hatchery fish, particularly males, were more timid and submissive. Consequently, hatchery males had only 62 percent of the mating success of their wild brethren. Hatchery females had delayed breeding that often resulted in their death before all of their eggs could be deposited. The hatchery females also lost more eggs to nest destruction by other females. Furthermore, the disadvantages of hatchery fish became more severe with increasing

8. See Ian A. Fleming and Mart R. Gross, "Breeding Success of Hatchery and Wild Coho Salmon (*Oncorhynchus kisutch*) in Competition."

density, that is, the hatchery fish's performance became even more anemic as the number of fish packed into a given area increased.

The implications of hatchery fish's inherent weaknesses have two worrisome implications with respect to wild salmon populations. First, it now appears that hatchery fish are unlikely to be very effective in rebuilding or enhancing native populations. They simply are not tough enough. Second, hatchery fish will almost certainly interbreed with wild fish and in so doing pass on their inferior genes to future generations. This movement of genes from one distinct population (or species) to another is called introgression. Introgression can lead to a range of genetic effects, including the creation of new species or the alteration of existing ones. In this case, the risk is that introgression might introduce some of the inadaptive hatchery genes into wild fish, thus further diminishing the prospects for wild populations. The extent to which introgression may already have occurred is difficult to determine. One recent survey of the literature on various salmonids concluded that the degree of introgression of hatchery into natural populations ranged from 0 percent to 100 percent at different sites, with good evidence for at least some introgression in seventeen out of thirty-one studies reviewed.[9]

The take-home message with respect to salmon is that the spectacular runs of Lewis and Clark's time are long gone from the rivers of Washington, Oregon, and California and probably will never return. There is something of a myth among well-intentioned conservationists and politicians that we can bring them back if we just invest enough in technological fixes. To bring things into focus, consider the discouraging but insightful words of Robert Lackey, a senior fisheries biologist

9. Ian A. Fleming and Erik Petersson, "The Ability of Released, Hatchery Salmonids to Breed and Contribute to the Natural Productivity of Wild Populations," 75.

with the Environmental Protection Agency who is leading salmon-restoration research:

> Restoring runs of wild salmon to the Pacific Northwest to levels that will support substantial fishing will not happen if current trajectories continue. Dramatic changes in salmon trends would have to occur if restoration had any chance of success. Society has yet to make the changes necessary for the restoration of wild salmon in appreciable numbers. . . . [M]ost stocks of wild salmon in the Pacific Northwest likely will remain at their current low levels or continue to decline in spite of costly restoration efforts. . . . Although few people appear to be happy with the present situation and a strong majority publicly professes support for maintaining wild salmon, there is little indication that society is inclined to confront the fundamental agents of the decline. Those causes deal with both individual life style and sheer numbers of people. Thus, it is likely that society will continue to chase the illusion that *wild* salmon runs can be restored without massive changes in the number, lifestyle, and philosophy of the human occupants of the western United States and Canada.[10]

At least we still have Alaska . . . and Kamchatka. It appears that Lewis was on to something when he suggested that the Columbia basin was not capable of supporting settlement except for perhaps forty to fifty thousand people in Oregon's Willamette Valley (as we will see in Chapter 10).

10. Lackey, "Restoring Wild Salmon," 91.

CHAPTER 7

❧

Clark's Nutcracker and Lewis's Woodpecker

A lthough Lewis arguably won the lottery with respect to having his name associated with the most fascinating and attractive plants (for example, *Lewisia rediviva* [bitterroot] and *Mimulus lewisii* [Lewis's monkey-flower]), Clark got the better deal when it came to bird names. True, Lewis's woodpecker is a beautiful bird, but it fares poorly compared to the miraculous Clark's nutcracker (*Nucifraga columbiana*), a bird so brainy as to completely invalidate the disparaging concept of "bird brain." This bird was first described by Clark on the same day and at the same location (along the Lemhi River in Idaho) as bitterroot, August 22, 1805. Clark wrote, "I Saw to day Bird of the wood pecker kind which fed on Pine burs its Bill and tale white the wings black every other part of a light brown, and about the Size of a robin."

As was often the case, both captains offered the same description nearly verbatim in their journals. In this case, it appears that Clark was the initial observer and that Lewis copied him, the reverse of the normal order. It seems unlikely that Lewis, being the astute naturalist that he was, would think this bird was a woodpecker if he had seen it himself. Nutcrackers are corvids (as are jays, crows, and ravens), and Lewis uses the term for the *Corvus* genus appropriately many times throughout the journals, including later, on May 28, 1806, when he gets a chance to examine this bird more closely:

> Since my arrival here I have killed several birds of the cor-
> vus genus of a kind found only in the rocky mountains and
> their neighbourhood. I first met with this bird above the three
> forks of the Missouri and saw them on the hights of the rocky
> Mountains but never before had an opportunity of examining
> them closely. the small corvus discribed at Fort Clatsop [the
> gray jay] is a different speceis, tho' untill now I had taken it
> to be the same, this is much larger and has a loud squawling
> note something like the mewing of a cat. the beak of this bird
> is 1 inches long, is proportionably large, black and of the form
> which characterizes the genus. the upper exceeds the under
> chap a little. the head and neck are also proportionably large.
> the eye full and reather prominent, the iris dark brown and
> puple black. it is about the size and somewhat the form of the
> Jaybird tho reather rounder or more full in the body. the tail is
> four and a half inches in length, composed of 12 feathers near-
> ly of the same length. the head neck and body of this bird are
> of a dove colour. the wings are black except the extremities of
> six large fathers ocupying the middle joint of the wing which
> are white. the under disk of the wing is not of the shining or
> grossy black which marks it's upper surface. the two feathers in
> the center of the tail are black as are the two adjacent feathers
> for half their width the ballance are of a pure white. the feet
> and legs are black and imbricated with wide scales. the nails
> are black and remarkably long and sharp, also much curved. it
> has four toes on each foot of which one is in the rear and three
> in front. the toes are long particularly that in the rear. this bird

Fig. 7.1. Clark's nutcracker (*Nucifraga columbiana*). Photo by G. Armistead/ Vireo.

feeds on the seed of the pine and also on insects. it resides in the rocky mountains at all seasons of the year, and in many parts is the only bird to be found.

The common and scientific name was assigned later by pioneer ornithologist Alexander Wilson (1766–1813). The Scottish-born Wilson was living in Philadelphia in 1806 and was engaged to document the birds of the Expedition just as Frederick Pursh was for plants. Wilson sketched and named three new birds from specimens that Lewis and Clark brought back: Clark's nutcracker (which he called Clark's crow, fig. 7.1), western tanager, and Lewis's woodpecker. He also sketched and named the magpie, but it turned out to be the same species as the magpie found in Eurasia.

Lewis was correct in his observation that Clark's nutcracker eats pine seeds. The particular pine in question is whitebark pine (*Pinus albicaulis*), and therein lies the story of why this bird is so fascinating. Whitebark pine is a high-elevation pine, often the last species to drop out as one ascends above timberline (fig. 7.2). Whitebark pine is a type of stone pine, so called because the seeds are large, heavy, and clunky, as opposed to other pines in which the seeds are small and winged to facilitate aerial dispersal. One seed of whitebark pine weighs around 175 milligrams, compared to 5 milligrams for lodgepole pine, a typical wind-dispersed species.[1] Stone pine seeds are dispersed by animals. In North America, this job is taken on by Clark's nutcracker and the pinyon jay of the southwestern United States. Similar nutcrackers exist in other parts of the world where stone pines are found, including Japan, Siberia, and Europe. Stone pines depend almost entirely on nutcrackers for seed dispersal, and nutcrackers depend almost entirely on pine seeds for food. It is a powerful and compelling example of the ecological concept of mutualism—the relationship between two different species in which both partners benefit from the partnership. In the case of the stone pines and nutcracker, the association is obligate, that is, each partner HAS to have the other in order to survive. Whitebark pine seeds are so chunky that they are not going anywhere without the birds to spread them around. Furthermore, the cones are tough and woody and do not open up on their own as most other pinecones do. Nutcrackers have a long, chisel-like bill that they use to pry open the cones and extract the seeds (fig. 7.3). The cones are not shed from the trees, but rather remain attached to the branches so as to present an easy target for nutcrackers. Once the seeds are out of the cone, the nutcrackers can store many dozens of seeds in their voluminous sublingual

---

1. Ronald M. Lanner, *Made for Each Other: A Symbiosis of Birds and Pines,* 28.

Fig. 7.2. Windswept whitebark pine at timberline near North Sister in the Oregon Cascade Range. Photo by the author.

Fig. 7.3. Cones of whitebark pine, which are two to three inches long. A nutcracker has broken open the cone on the right and removed some of the seeds. Courtesy of Diana Tomback (http://www.whitebark-found.org).

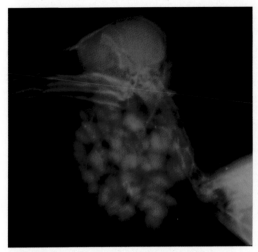

Fig. 7.4. X-ray view of Clark's nutcracker with its sublingual pouch filled with twenty-eight pinyon-pine seeds. These seeds are considerably larger than whitebark-pine seeds, of which more than one hundred may be accommodated at one time. Photo courtesy of S. B. Vander Wall.

(beneath the tongue) pouch (fig. 7.4). When they are satisfied that they have a sufficient load, the birds will fly off and stash the seeds in an underground cache for later retrieval.

The amount of seeds that are stored by these birds can be staggering. Several scientists have independently estimated that a single nutcracker will store twenty-two to thirty-five thousand seeds a year.[2] Since nutcrackers live year-round at high elevations, they rely on these seed caches to get them through the hard times. The seeds have a high fat content and thus about as much energy, pound for pound, as pure butter. This rich food helps the birds to breed in early spring while snow still covers much of the area.

Practically all regeneration of whitebark pines requires seed planting by nutcrackers, though ground squirrels and a few other animals can play a supporting role. In a good seed year, a typical acre of prime alpine landscape may be loaded with more than ten thousand neatly planted pine seeds. Less well-intentioned seed predators will have a

2. Ibid., 45–46.

hard time finding them. Once the seeds germinate, the buried location helps to prevent early dehydration.

Nutcrackers have an enlarged hippocampus—that region of the brain that deals with spatial recognition and memory. These brainy birds use visual cues to remember the location of a substantial portion of their stored seeds for up to ten months. Even if most of the seeds are eventually reclaimed and eaten, some will be overlooked and go on to establish the next generation of pines. The patchy distribution of seed caches results in landscape-scale effects in which the trees form clumps or "islands." This is one of the most distinguishing features of timberline settings in the Pacific Northwest. The tree islands provide refuges from the harsh alpine conditions where many other species, such as mountain hemlock and numerous shrubs, can get started and prosper.

Clark's nutcracker appears to be in for some hard times to come. The problem can be traced to a fungus (*Cronartium ribicola*) that causes white pine blister rust (fig. 7.5). This nonnative fungus was introduced accidentally to North America around 1922 with devastating results for all white pines (those with five needles per cluster or technically known as a "fascicle"). White pine blister rust has caused more damage and cost more to control that any other disease of conifers in North America. The victims include a range of large, stately, and extremely valuable timber trees such as eastern white pine, western white pine, and sugar pine as well as the more humble whitebark pine. Although natural stands of the timber species have been severely impacted, extensive research has led to the development of new lines that are resistant to the fungus. The future for these high-value species appears to be fairly rosy, at least in managed stands. But whitebark pine is a gnarly runt with no commercial value, so there has been little driving force to develop resistant lines. In areas such as Crater Lake National Park, 26 percent of the whitebark pines have already been lost. In Glacier National

Fig. 7.5. A stem of whitebark pine with a fruiting canker of blister rust. Courtesy of Diana Tomback (http://www.whitebarkfound.org).

Park, mortality was already up to 90 percent by 1990.[3] Although there has been some recent research directed at this problem, it is not clear whether help will arrive in time. It may not really matter anyway, because, as global climate change progresses, vegetation zones are predicted to shift upward in elevation. For a timberline species such as whitebark pine, there is simply not much real estate left for them to retreat to. The pines and their associated nutcrackers may literally be squeezed off the top of the mountains.

What about Lewis's contribution to avian nomenclature? Lewis's woodpecker (*Melanerpes lewis*, literally, "Lewis's black creeper") may not be quite as fascinating as Clark's nutcracker, but it is still an

3. Michael P. Murray and Mary Rasmussen, "Status of Whitebark Pine in Crater Lake National Park," n.p.; Katherine C. Kendall and Stephen F. Arno, "Whitebark Pine: An Important but Endangered Wildlife Resource."

Fig. 7.6. Lewis's woodpecker (*Melaner-pes lewis*). Photo by J. Fuhrman/ Vireo.

impressive and beautiful bird, with its large size and rosy-pink belly (fig. 7.6). Unlike most other woodpeckers, it does not hammer away at wood to obtain boring insects. Instead, it snatches bugs from the air or from the surface of vegetation. It also has a fondness for fruits and nuts, especially acorns that it collects right off the tree. It tucks

Fig. 7.7. Sketch of the original specimen of Lewis's woodpecker drawn by Charles Willson Peale, a prominent artist, naturalist, and Phildelphia museum curator. Peale was also noted for his portraits of American presidents and of Lewis and Clark. Copyright American Philosophical Society.

the acorn into a handy crevice in a tree trunk, where the acorn can be hammered open or stored for later use. Lewis's woodpecker has a patchy distribution and can be irruptive, that is, prone to irregular increases, from one year to the next, thus a traveler just like its namesake (fig. 7.7).

A specimen of Lewis's woodpecker collected by Lewis currently resides at the Museum of Comparative Zoology at Harvard University and apparently is the only zoological specimen from the Expedition that has survived to modern times. Lewis proved to be as keen

an observer of birds as he was of plants. He provided a long description of this woodpecker that proves his bona fides as a naturalist on
several points: (1) "It is a distinct species of woodpecker" (July 20,
1805). Lewis was familiar enough with all known woodpeckers from
the East that he knew from a fleeting glance that this was a new species. (2) "Flys a good deel like the jay bird" (July 20, 1805). Almost
all woodpeckers fly with a characteristic undulating flight pattern in
which the bird rises with each wing beat and sinks in between beats.
It is a reliable field feature that all bird-watchers use to spot woodpeckers from a distance. But Lewis's woodpecker does not do this,
and Lewis spotted the difference right away. Nowadays, this bird is
sometimes called a "crow woodpecker" in deference to its large size
and corvidlike flying habits. And (3) "It has four toes on each foot of
which two are in rear and two in front" (May 27, 1806). Toe number
and arrangement are important characteristics of woodpeckers that
modern ornithologists focus on. This unique arrangement of toes is
an important feature of woodpeckers that helps provide stability on
vertical tree trunks. (Most birds have three toes forward, one facing
backward.)

CHAPTER 8

Greater Sage-grouse and Sage

THE SAGE AND THE GROUSE SEEM MADE FOR EACH OTHER.

—Rachel Carson, *Silent Spring*

When Norwegians or Swedes get bored on those bleak, cold spring days, they may go to see a play, or lek (rhymes with "peck"), as they call it. So do some of their birds, particularly grouse. When grouse go to a lek, they have a different agenda in mind. They are looking for a mate. Ornithologists use the term *lek* to indicate the gathering places where grouse congregate for a highly ritualized mating display in which the male puffs up his chest and calls insistently to attract attention (fig. 8.1). For the greater sage-grouse of the American West, the call sounds like a drowning rooster on steroids, in an alien, gurgly sort of way. The hens listen carefully and pick out their favorite (fig. 8.2). For grouse (but not Norwegians), loud and showy is the way to mating success. Usually, the top male ends up with all the action, and all the other males get an honorable mention at best.

Lewis and Clark saw numerous grouse species on their trek west, but largest and most intriguing was the greater sage-grouse (*Centro-*

Fig. 8.1. Greater sage-grouse, male (*left and background*) and female (*right*). Photo courtesy of Neil Losin (http://www. neillosin.com/).

Fig. 8.2. A robotic, radio-controlled female greater sage-grouse ("fembot") being used by Gail Patricelli and coworkers at the University of California at Davis. The robot is equipped with a microphone and video camera and is mounted on a model-train track so that its position can be moved within the lek. The goal is to quantify how directionality shapes male display behaviors and female choice. Photo courtesy of Neil Losin (http://www. neillosin.com/).

cercus urophasianus), which they called the "Cock of the Plains." Paul Cutright credits the Expedition with discovering five gallinaceous (roughly, chickenlike) birds in addition to the greater sage-grouse: the Columbian sharp-tailed grouse, the dusky grouse, Franklin's grouse, the Oregon ruffed grouse, and the mountain quail. More recently, grouse experts Fred Zwickel and Mike Schroeder have provided a more detailed analysis of the Expedition's sightings and the modern taxonomy of grouse.[1] In addition to its fascinating behavior and showy appearance, the greater sage-grouse has qualities that link it to the essential character of the American West (for instance, spectacular success in the midst of arid bleakness) in a way quite similar to the Expedition's flagship plant species—*Lewisia, Clarkia,* and *Calochortus.* The fates of western ecosystems in general and greater sage-grouse are closely linked and well worth close examination.

Lewis provided a detailed description of the greater sage-grouse on March 2, 1806, while camped at Fort Clatsop:

> The Cock of the Plains is found in the plains of Columbia and are in Great abundance from the entrance of the S. E. fork of the Columbia to that of Clark's river.[2] this bird is about 2/3rds the size of a turkey. the beak is large short curved and convex. the upper exceeding the lower chap. the nostrils are large and the b[e]ak black. the colour is an uniform mixture of dark brown reather bordeing on a dove colour, redish and yellowish brown with some small black specks. in this mixture the dark brown prevails and has a slight cast of the dove colour at a little distance. the wider side of the large feathers of the wings are of a dark brown only. the tail is composed of 19 feathers

1. See Cutright, *Lewis and Clark,* 429–36; and Zwickel and Schroeder, "Grouse of the Lewis and Clark Expedition, 1803 to 1806."
2. Today's Bitterroot River.

of which that in the center is the longest, and the remaining 9 on each side deminish by pairs as they receede from the center; that is any one feather is equal in length to one equa distant from the center of the tail on the oposite side. the tail when foalded comes to a very sharp point and appears long in proportion to the body. in the act of flying the tail resembles that of a wild pigeon. tho' the motion of the wings is much that of the pheasant and Grouse. they have four toes on each foot of which the hinder one is short. the leg is covered with feathers about half the distance between the knee and foot. when the wing is expanded there are wide opening between it's feathers the plumeage being so narrow that it does not extend from one quill to the other. the wings are also proportionably short, reather more so than those of the pheasant or grouse. the habits of this bird are much the same as those of the grouse. only that the food of this fowl is almost entirely that of the leaf and buds of the pulpy leafed thorn; nor do I ever recollect seeing this bird but in the neighbourhood of that shrub. they sometimes feed on the prickley pear. the gizzard of it is large and much less compressed and muscular than in most fowls; in short it resembles a maw quite as much as a gizzard. when they fly they make a cackling noise something like the dunghill fowl. . . . [T]he flesh of the cock of the Plains is dark, and only tolerable in point of flavor. I do not think it as good as either the Pheasant or Grouse.—it is invariably found in the plains.—The feathers about it's head are pointed and stif some hairs about the base of the beak. feathers short fine and stif about the ears.

Lewis was apparently using his downtime at Fort Clatsop to get caught up on his journals, since greater sage-grouse were not present in the vicinity. He was working from memory and, perhaps, notes. As the modern name implies, greater sage-grouse are found around sagebrush. There is no sagebrush within one hundred miles of Fort

Clatsop. Sagebrush is a plant of the arid lands east of the Cascade Range, whereas Fort Clatsop is right in the heart of the soggy temperate rain forest of western Oregon. But Lewis and Clark were in a dash for the coast when they passed through sagebrush country a few months earlier, so they did not take the time to record the details of the grouse natural history. Perhaps it is this lag period that explains Lewis's rare (though minor) error of observation when he states that this bird eats the "leaf and buds of the pulpy leafed thorn," by which he means greasewood (*Sarcobatus vermiculatus*). Greater sage-grouse eat sagebrush, not greasewood. To be fair, sagebrush is almost always in abundance wherever greasewood is found—at least in the regions through which Lewis was traveling (fig. 8.3).

This propensity to eat sagebrush is one of the more remarkable aspects of sage-grouse biology. Although a number of mammals (deer, elk, cattle, horses, and others) will eat some sagebrush if they have no alternatives, the palatability is rated as poor to fair at best, and the animals will seldom eat much of it. Sagebrush is loaded with a host of bitter, terpentine-like chemicals ("terpenoids") whose evolutionary function is to prevent herbivory. There are at least twenty-eight terpenoids in sagebrush, with camphor being the predominant form.[3] Despite the name, sagebrush is *not* related to the common sage found in herb gardens. Common or garden sage (*Salvia officinalis*) is in the mint family (Lamiaceae), whereas sagebrush is in the sunflower family (Asteraceae). Camphor makes a pretty decent bug or moth repellent but an extremely poor choice for culinary embellishment. You will find about 4 percent camphor in common sports liniments such as Bengay, but odds are you would not be tempted to try it for dessert. But a greater sage-grouse would. In fact, they

3. See Hans A. Buttkus, Robert J. Bose, and Duncan A. Shearer, "Terpenes in Essential Oil of Sagebrush (*Artemisia tridentata*)."

Fig. 8.3. *Left:* Flowers and foliage of sagebrush (*Artemisia tridentata*). *Above:* Sagebrush habitat; bitterbrush (*Purshia tridentata*) and cheatgrass (*Bromus tectorum*) are also present. Copyright 2007 Mark Turner.

pretty much insist on sagebrush to the exclusion of all else. Lewis's observation that the flesh of greater sage-grouse is "only tolerable in point of flavor" can be attributed to the camphor-rich diet.

Other gallinaceous birds (for example, chickens, turkeys, quail, and other grouse) eat mostly seeds that they grind up in their crop, that is, gizzard, with the assistance of small stones that they swallow for that purpose. A crop is a hard mass of muscle with considerable crunching power through which the seeds pass on their way to the stomach. As Lewis astutely observed, the greater sage-grouse's gizzard is unique—a flabby sack hardly worthy of being called a gizzard at all. They do not need one, since all they eat is soft sagebrush leaves and buds . . . that and the odd bug or two, mostly in the summer.

The mating behavior of greater sage-grouse is strikingly bizarre. This bird is one of the classic examples of a lekking bird. Leks often range in size up to one hectare (roughly the area of a square, with each side the length of a football field), with successful leks being reused year after year.[4] The action at leks typically begins in late February and reaches a peak in April before tapering off in May. If there is a full moon, the males may attend their leks all night, but more often they gear up an hour or so before sunrise and remain active for two to four hours per day. Each male stakes out his own territory of thirteen to one hundred square meters from which he woos females by performing an elaborate display called a "strut." A strutting male will fan out his tail feathers, raise his head, and erect the showy feathers on the sides of his neck. He inflates his esophageal air sac to the incredible volume of three liters and quickly deflates it to make his distinct tympanic sound. Territorial disputes between adjacent males are settled with false charges and wing fighting but seldom with any

---

4. See R. Haven Wiley, "Territoriality and Non-random Mating in Sage Grouse (*Centrocercus urophasianus*)."

serious injury. Strutting males mean business and will expend energy at a rate four times that of the basal resting metabolic rate, a level that corresponds to the absolute physiological limit.[5] The females will congregate in dense packs at selected sites called mating centers that are roughly five meters in diameter and within the territory of the dominant male.

Greater sage-grouse males make prolific lovers but deadbeat dads. A successful one may mate with up to thirty females in a three-hour period, but that is the limit of his contribution to parenting. The females fly off to remote sites to nest and raise the young with no assistance from the male.

There is no mention in the journals that Lewis and Clark observed the courtship displays of the greater sage-grouse on their leks. Certainly, on the return trip, in April 1806, the timing would have been right as they passed through eastern Washington and into Idaho.

An active grouse lek is one of the more spectacular sites in nature. Since the same site is used year after year, it is possible to go out in the field with a knowledgeable guide with a high probability of seeing the real thing. A mini-ecotourism business is flourishing in the West as well as in Scandinavia in which bird-watchers are provided with just that opportunity. It is well worth rising at three in the morning to see. Considering the precarious state of greater sage-grouse, I would recommend doing it sooner rather than later. As the map in figure 8.4 shows, the distribution of these magnificent birds has declined markedly, especially along the Columbia River, where Lewis and Clark traveled.

Greater sage-grouse these days face many of the same problems of the sagebrush ecosystem in general across the West: overgrazing,

---

5. See Sandra L. Vehrencamp, Jack W. Bradbury, and Robert M. Gibson, "The Energetic Cost of Display in Male Sage Grouse."

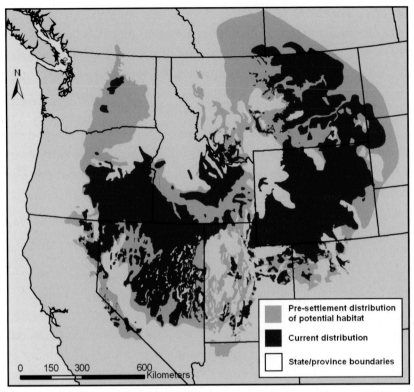

Fig. 8.4. Historic and current (1999) range of greater sage-grouse in the western United States. From Mike Schroeder, Washington Department of Fish and Wildlife.

habitat degradation and fragmentation, invasive weeds, conversion of habitat to cropland, oil and gas development, and off-road vehicles. They once numbered about two million but are now down to less than 10 percent of that figure.[6] The greater sage-grouse has emerged as a key indicator of ecosystem health in sagebrush country in much the same way that the spotted owl has for big-timber country on the

6. Scott Weidensaul, "Sage Grouse Strut Their Stuff."

west side of the Cascade Range. The U.S. Fish and Wildlife Service recently decided not to list greater sage-grouse for protection under the Endangered Species Act. The decision provoked considerable ire among conservationists, as reported by Felicity Barringer of the *New York Times* on December 5, 2004:

> The scientific opinions of a Bush administration appointee at the Interior Department with no background in wildlife biology were provided as part of the source material for the panel of Fish and Wildlife Service biologists and managers who recommended against giving the greater sage-grouse protection under the endangered species act. . . . The sage-grouse, whose habitat overlaps areas of likely oil and gas deposits across states like Wyoming and Montana, would likely become an economic headache to the energy and cattle industries if it were listed. A listing can trigger extensive regulation and increase costs and delays. . . .
>
> . . . On whether sage grouse need sagebrush to survive during the winter, the career biologists wrote: "Sage-grouse depend entirely on sagebrush throughout the winter for both food and cover." Ms. MacDonald [the political appointee] wrote: "I believe that is an overstatement, as they will eat other stuff if it's available."[7]

Monitoring and protection of sage-grouse will remain on the agenda for conservation biologists with the hope for more progressive oversight in the future.

Sagebrush has quite a bit going for it on its own even without the grouse. Taken in a broad sense, the genus for sagebrush (*Artemisia*)

---

7. Barringer, "Interior Official and Federal Biologists Clash on Danger to Bird," *New York Times,* December 5, 2004. Ms. MacDonald eventually resigned under congressional pressure three years later.

is very successful and widespread, with about three hundred species in the Northern Hemisphere and in South America. Ancient Egyptians were familiar with a form of *Artemisia* (*A. absinthium*) called wormwood because of its ability to rid the body of parasitic worms. Wormwood is mentioned many places in the Bible. Pliny the Elder (the Roman encyclopedist and author) noted that wormwood "taken on voyages averts sea-sickness; worn under a cummerbund it prevents swelling of the groin. It promotes sleep if inhaled or secretly placed under a patient's head ... amongst clothes ... keeps off moths. . . . [M]ixed with oil, wormwood drives away gnats when the body is rubbed all over with it. . . . [W]hen ignited, its smoke repels gnats. Ink mixed with wormwood protects writings from mice."[8]

Lewis was familiar with the genus that he variously called wild hyssop, wild hop, wormwood, or sage. Curiously, although Lewis and Clark collected five species of *Artemisia* (*cana, dracunculus, frigida, longifolia,* and *ludoviciana*), they did not return with specimens of *A. tridentata*, which is by far the most common of the lot. It is likely that this species was collected but the specimens lost in the spring floods that destroyed so many other specimens at the cache left near the Great Falls of the Missouri. On the whole, this genus received only slight, passing attention in the journals. A typical example is found in Lewis's entry from April 29, 1805: "Saw a bay horse in a beautiful Smooth plain on the N. S. where we Saw a great quantity of wild Hop [sagebrush] Growing we Suppose that this horse had Strayed from Some Savages."

As usual, sagebrush gets a brief mention, and then it's off to something else. It is curious that such an abundant plant as sagebrush would consistently attract so little comment. Perhaps Lewis thought it was not particularly noteworthy because it was of low value for

8. Pliny the Elder, *Natural History*, bk. 27.

food for man or beast and was so familiar to him already from re-lated species in the East. His best description was offered up on April 14, 1805, when he wrote: "On these hills many aromatic herbs are seen; resembling in taste, smel and appearance, the sage, hysop, wormwood, southernwood . . . the one resembling the camphor in taste and smell, rising to the hight of 2 or 3 feet." It turns out that Lewis was a pretty good chemist in addition to naturalist. Scientists nowadays would routinely use a gas chromatograph-mass spectrom-eter to identify camphor in sagebrush. Lewis spotted the camphor in sagebrush with a nose-a-metric analysis.

Sagebrush was more successful in attracting the attention of later authors such as Mark Twain, who wrote in *Roughing It*, "Sagebrush is very fair fuel, but as a vegetable it is a distinguished failure. Noth-ing can abide the taste of it but the jackass and his illegitimate child the mule. But their testimony to its nutritiousness is worth nothing, for they will eat pine knots, or anthracite coal, or brass filings, or lead pipe, or old bottles, or anything that comes handy, and then go off looking as grateful as if they had had oysters for dinner."

It should be mentioned that sagebrush was of considerable utility to the Indians of the Intermountain West. If they got hungry enough, they could boil the leaves and eat them, though they still remained bitter and of marginal nutrition. Sagebrush was used commonly as an antirheumatic, antiseptic, disinfectant, febrifuge, poultice, and seda-tive. It was also used to treat digestive disorders, sore throats, pneu-monia, colds, and bronchitis. The fibrous bark was used for weaving mats, baskets, sandals, and many other everyday items. The foliage and branches were used to construct crude temporary shelters. All things considered, sagebrush was one of the most heavily used and versatile plants that the Indians had.

Modern science can confirm that at least some of these medicinal uses had a sound basis. Camphor and many other terpenoids that are present in sagebrush do indeed kill bacteria and fungi. Some species of *Artemisia* (though apparently not *A. tridentata*) produce a chemical that is effective in treating malaria and may be on the verge of replacing quinine (another plant product) for that purpose due to the alarming rise of quinine-resistant strains of the malaria parasite. And who among westerners would dispute that the aroma of fresh sagebrush, especially after a summer rain, is indeed delightful and restorative to the soul?

The chemicals produced by sagebrush may well have benefits to the plant beyond just that of deterring would-be mammal or insect herbivores. Some of those chemicals are capable of causing allelopathy—the chemical warfare in which one plant produces toxins that inhibit the growth of competing species. This phenomenon is covered in more detail later in this book (in Chapter 10) with respect to knapweed.

Even more fascinating is the apparent ability of some of these chemicals to act as signals in which plants alert their neighbors that evildoers are lurking nearby. Sagebrush foliage emits a volatile chemical called methyl jasmonate.[9] The levels emitted rise dramatically in response to mechanical damage of the leaves such as that caused by munching caterpillars. This chemical wafts through the air where it is detected by other plants, where alarm bells are set off. The receiving plant gets the message that herbivores are at work in the area, and so the plant will increase its production of its own defensive compounds even though that particular plant has not actually been damaged. It is an elegant system that conserves the plant's limited resources. Why waste carbon and energy making defense compounds when you don't need them? Sagebrush plants can communicate to other sagebrush plants in this fashion, in which case a 50 percent reduction in her-

9. Richard Karban et al., "The Specificity of Eavesdropping on Sagebrush by Other Plants."

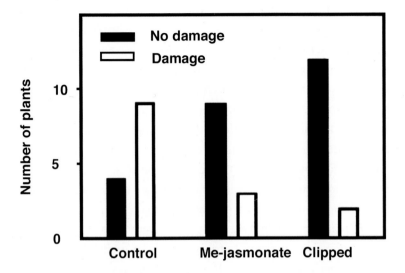

Fig. 8.5. Eavesdropping by tobacco plants on sagebrush. Herbivore damage was recorded in tobacco plants that were exposed to an atmosphere containing a known standard of volatile methyl jasmonate (*center pair of bars*) or grown in the vicinity of sagebrush plants that had been clipped (*right pair of bars*) in order to induce the production of methyl jasmonate by the sagebrush. The control plants (*left pair of bars*) received no alert signal and thus were caught unawares and suffered more damage. From Karban, Huntzinger, and McCall, "Specificity of Eavesdropping."

bivory of the neighboring plants has been observed. Other species may even "eavesdrop" on sagebrush and in so doing learn when it is expedient to turn on their own defenses (fig. 8.5).

Is it any wonder that sagebrush makes up more than 90 percent of the plant biomass at many sites in the West? Is there any reason to be concerned about the future for sagebrush? It looks like they can pretty much take care of themselves. That is true enough under natural conditions, but methyl jasmonate is not much defense against a herd of heavy-footed cattle or the farmer's tractor. And recently introduced weeds such as knapweed have chemical arsenals that easily trump sagebrush's. Last, humans have introduced another complicating factor into the sagebrush story: fire suppression. Even though fire temporarily destroys sagebrush, too little fire can be even worse, because it allows juniper trees to displace the sagebrush on a long-term basis. Junipers may look nice, but nobody likes them much except for deer and cattle who appreciate the shade. Junipers are even more useless than sagebrush for food, and they suck the land dry of valuable moisture that could otherwise be used to grow something more palatable. At least junipers are native, and the "berries" (actually fleshy cones) can be used to make gin. Of course, like any native plant, it does have a place in western landscapes, but it is not a place that is very friendly to sagebrush or greater sage-grouse. Perhaps juniper's most outstanding quality is that finally we have something that environmentalists, ranchers, range scientists, birders, and land managers alike can agree to disparage.

CHAPTER 9

Fossils

J efferson had a long-standing interest in fossils and the missing megafauna of North America, as discussed in Chapter 1. His expectation that the Corps of Discovery might encounter living mammoths or giant ground sloths was of course unfulfilled, but there were some interesting related developments that were not anticipated. To appreciate this, one needs to realize that the concepts of geologic time, extinction, evolution, and natural selection were unknown at the time of the Expedition. A few scientists were just beginning to suspect that the earth might be older than a few thousand years—the age supported by Bible scholars of the time. Charles Darwin would not be born until 1809—the same year that Lewis died. Dinosaurs were not discovered until 1842. But Lewis and Clark were nothing if not skilled (and lucky) in operating in a vacuum of knowledge. As was so often the case, they were rewarded by their diligence in observation. On at least two separate occasions they saw and collected what we now realize were dinosaur fossils.

The first discovery occurred on September 10, 1804, as the Expedition was making its way through South Dakota. While on Cedar

Island, in the middle of the Missouri River, they stumbled onto the fossil remains of the backbone, teeth, and ribs of a plesiosaur, an ocean-dwelling dinosaur of the Mesozoic era. Clark and three other journalists (Gass, Whitehouse, and Ordway) all noted the finding in their journals, although they assumed they had found a "monstrous large fish" (Whitehouse). These fossils are now in the Smithsonian Institution in Washington, D.C. Here is what Clark had to say about it:

> A Cloudy morning Set out early under a Gentle Breeze from the S E. . . . [A]t 10 1/2 miles passed the lower pt. of Ceder Island Situated in a bend to the L. S. this Island is about 2 miles long Covered with red Ceder, the river is verry Shallow opsd. this Island—below the Island on the top of a ridge we found a back bone with the most of the entire laying Connected for 45 feet those bones are petrified, Some teeth & ribs also Connected.

The explorers' second encounter with fossils occurred on July 25, 1806, near Pompeys Pillar in Montana. Clark wrote:

> I employed himself in getting pieces of the rib of a fish which was Semented within the face of the rock this rib is about 3 inchs in Secumpherance about the middle. . . . [I]t is 3 feet in length tho a part of the end appears to have been broken off I have Several peces of this rib the bone is neither decayed nor petrified but very rotten. the part which I could not get out maybe Seen, it is about 6 or 7 Miles below Pompey's Tower in the face of the Lard. [larboard] Clift about 20 feet above the water.

The samples have not survived, so the identity of this "fish" is uncertain. This rock strata has turned out to be incredibly rich in fossils and is now called the Hell Creek Formation. The formation is probably the most studied of any site in North America with respect to the fauna of the Cretaceous period (144–65 million years ago). Common dinosaurs found here include hadrosaurs ("duck-billed dinosaurs"), *Triceratops*, *Albertosaurus*, and *Tyrannosaurus rex*. Had fate been kinder, we might have come to know the tyrant-lizard king as *Clarkiosaurus rex*. At any rate, the observations of Clark are often cited in paleontology texts as one of the first reported finds of dinosaur bones anywhere in the world.

The explorers had one other notable encounter with ancient fossils. On August 6, 1804, Patrick Gass found an upper jaw bone, complete with teeth, on the Soldier River in present-day Harrison County, Iowa. This specimen survives today at the Academy of Natural Sciences in Philadelphia (fig. 9.1). There is no mention of it in any of the journals, but the specimen still bears a label, in Lewis's hand, that reads, "Petrified jaw bone of a fish or some other anamal found in a cavern a few miles distant from the Missouri—S. side of the river."

In this case, Lewis nearly got it right. It was a fish, or more accurately a large "sword-eel" from the Late Cretaceous. Confusion has

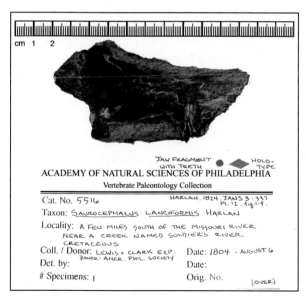

Fig. 9.1. Jaw fragment and label from the "sword-eel" fossil collected by the Lewis and Clark Expedition. Photo by Mike Everhart, Oceans of Kansas Paleontology.

followed this specimen through the centuries. It was misidentified by Richard Harlan in 1824[1] and assigned to a new genus and species—*Saurocephalus lanciformis*—thus classifying it as a type of marine reptile related to ichthyosaurs. Later scientists decided it was clearly a fish, not a reptile, and the naming and renaming have continued into recent times, keeping several modern paleontologists duly occupied. Regardless of its taxonomic disposition, this specimen remains noteworthy as the first fossil to be collected and described from the Niobrara Formation, an incredibly productive treasure house of fossils (and oil) in Nebraska and surrounding states.

Jefferson's interests in fossils continued throughout his lifetime. In 1807, a year after the Expedition returned, he was back at it again. This time he sent Clark back to Big Bone Lick in Kentucky to see if he would have better luck collecting fossils. The Expedition had stopped there briefly on the way to St. Louis in 1803, but the specimens they shipped back were lost when the boat carrying them sank in the Mississippi, much to the frustration of Jefferson. Clark's return trip in 1807 was probably the first expedition in the United States organized for the purpose of vertebrate paleontology.

Early Euro-Americans had been collecting fossils at this site since 1739. Thousands of specimens were sent back to Europe for the leading naturalists of the time to examine. Clark employed a team of ten laborers. Even though earlier collectors had picked over many of the prime specimens, Clark's team was able to extricate about three hundred bones that he sent back to Jefferson. Most of these bones were from mastodons, but several other species were represented as well (table 9.1).

1. See Harlan, "On a New Fossil Genus of the Order Enalio Sauir (of Conybeare)"; and Mike Everhart, "Oceans of Kansas Paleontology: Fossils from the Late Cretaceous Western Interior Sea."

Table 9.1. Comparison of Clark's and the currently accepted identification of fossils collected at Big Bone Lick and returned to Jefferson in 1807	
Clark's identification	**Modern identification**
"Mammoth"	American mastodon (*Mammut americanum*)
"Eliphant"	Wooly mammoth (*Mammuthus primigenius*)
"Sheep or goat species"	Harlan's musk ox (*Bootherium bombifrons*)
"Horse"	Ancient horse (*Equus complicatus*)
"Buffalow Cow"	Ancient bison (*Bison antiquus*)
"Moose Deer" or "Elk"	Stag-moose (*Cervalces scotti*)

Jefferson was delighted with the haul. He sent part to the American Philosophical Society and some to the Muséum d'Histoire Naturelle in Paris. He also kept a few pieces for his personal collection that was displayed at Monticello. The specimens received much attention from Caspar Wistar, Jefferson's friend and noted anatomist, and other members of the American Philosophical Society. It was Wistar who a few years earlier had correctly surmised that Jefferson's *Megalonyx* (giant ground sloth) was most closely related to a sloth and not a "tiger-lion," as Jefferson had supposed. Wistar definitely knew his bones. Over the next few decades, the Big Bone Lick bones provided the basis for the fledgling science of paleontology in the United States.

The case of the Harlan's (or helmeted) musk ox is representative.[2] Clark was not sure what to call it, but his best guess ("sheep or goat")

2. See Academy of Natural Sciences, "Harlan's Musk Ox (*Bootherium bombifrons*)."

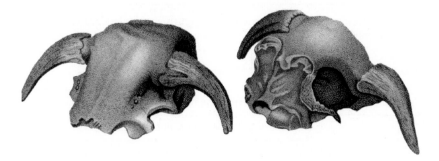

Fig. 9.2. Drawing of the skull of Harlan's musk ox as it appeared in Wistar's publication of 1818. Copyright American Philosophical Society.

is actually pretty close, since those animals are among their closest living relatives. Harlan's musk ox is another example of the megafauna that went extinct in the Late Pleistocene due, at least in part, to predation by humans. We now know that there were at least four species of musk ox in North America, some of which reached as far south as present-day Kansas. The tundra musk ox (*Ovibos mochatus*) managed to hold on to modern times, largely because it was fortunate to be in such remote areas (Greenland and northern Canada) that humans were not a significant threat.

Wistar's attention was drawn to the unusual skulls returned by Clark from his fossil foray in 1807, which Wistar described in an 1818 publication.[3] Wistar provided a detailed description as well as numerous figures, focusing his description on the manner in which the horns were attached to the skull (fig. 9.2). He made numerous comparisons to similar features in ox, deer, sheep, and bison. None of these were an exact match, forcing him to conclude his report

3. See Wistar, "An Account of Two Heads Found in the Morass, Called Big Lick, and Presented to the Society, by Mr. Jefferson."

with uncertainty: "Was not this animal allied to the bison?" In other words, the practice of ending scientific reports with the phrase "further research is called for" has been around for a long time. In this case, the correct identification and modern name were eventually provided in 1852 by Joseph Leidy, who can justly be called the father of American vertebrate paleontology.

Although you may not have heard of Caspar Wistar, you probably have heard of the plant that the noted English-born botanist Thomas Nuttall named after him—*Wisteria*. Nuttall got the spelling wrong, but the published misspelling has to stand uncorrected due to the International Code of Botanical Nomenclature. Once published, that's the way it is. Wistar also prepared a list of natural history questions for Lewis to examine during his Expedition. Unfortunately, that list was lost, so we do not know what it contained. If the list had survived, then Wistar's name would probably have a more prominent place in history, perhaps even conspicuous enough that Nuttall would have known how to spell it.

CHAPTER 10

Missing Pieces

Three animals stand out as the quintessential reflection of the spirit of the American West of pre-European time: the buffalo, grizzly bear, and gray wolf. All have nearly disappeared as meaningful forces in ecosystems in the lower forty-eight states with the exception of a few protected areas, notably Yellowstone National Park, an area that Lewis and Clark never visited. The fate of these animals is symbolic of our anthropocentric view of nature and the accompanying worldview that all natural resources are subject to exploitation for the ultimate benefit of humans. The extent to which these resources have been exploited never would have occurred to Lewis or Clark in their wildest imagination. Nature was simply there—a presumably inexhaustible resource. Consider Lewis's journal offering from May 5, 1805: "As usual saw a great quantity of game today; Buffaloe Elk and goats or Antelopes feeding in every direction; we kill whatever we wish, the buffaloe furnish us with fine veal and fat beef, we also have venison and beaver tales when we wish them; the flesh of the Elk and goat are less esteemed, and certainly are inferior. . . . The country is as yesterday beatifull in the extreme."

The captains were not naive, but they were a product of their time. They had no reason to anticipate the possible exhaustion of the nation's natural wealth. However, they did predict, along with Jefferson, that the West would eventually be settled and partly tamed. For instance, when Lewis passed the rich Willamette Valley on March 30, 1806, near what is now Portland, Oregon, he noted that "this valley would be copetent to the mantainance of 40 or 50 thousand souls if properly cultivated and is indeed the only desireable situation for a settlement which I have seen on the West side of the Rocky mountains." For the record, about 2.5 million people (and zero wolves or grizzly bears) now live in the Willamette Valley, and the number is likely to increase to 4 million by 2050.[1] Lewis was a bit off in his estimate, but nobody else saw it coming either.

Wolves were a part of everyday life for Lewis and Clark. They are mentioned literally hundreds of times in the journals. Lewis provides a particularly descriptive entry in his journal of May 5, 1805:

> Saw the carcases of many Buffaloe lying dead along the shore partially devoured by the wolves and bear. . . . Clark found a den of young wolves in the course of his walk today and also saw a great number of those anamals; they are very abundant in this quarter, and are of two species [coyote and gray wolf] the small woolf or burrowing dog of the praries are the inhabitants almost invariably of the open plains; they usually ascociate in bands of ten or twelve sometimes more and burrow near some pass or place much frequented by game; not being able alone

1. Willamette Valley Livability Forum, "Oregon's Willamette Valley: Facts and Figures," n.p.

to take deer or goat they are rarely ever found alone but hunt in bands; they frequently watch and seize their prey near their burrows; in these burrows they raise their young and to them they also resort when pursued; when a person approaches them they frequently bark, their note being precisely that of the small dog. they are of an intermediate size between that of the fox and dog, very active fleet and delicately formed; the years large erect and pointed the head long and pointed more like that of the fox; tale long <and bushey>; the hair and fur also resembles the fox tho' is much coarser and inferior. they are of a pale redish brown colour. the eye of a deep sea green colour small and piercing. their tallons are reather longer than those of the ordinary wolf or that common to the atlantic states, none of which are to be found in this quarter, nor I believe above the river Plat.—The large wooolf found here is not as large as those of the atlantic states. they were lower and <heaver> thicker made shorter leged. their colour which is not effected by the seasons, is a grey or blackish brown and every intermediate shade from that to a creen [cream] coloured white; these wolves resort the woodlands and are also found in the plains, but never take refuge in the ground or burrow so far as I have been able to inform myself. we scarcely see a gang of buffaloe without observing a parsel of those faithfull shepherds on their skirts in readiness to take care of the mamed & wounded. the large wolf never barks, but howls as those of the atlantic states do.

Despite Lewis's idyllic description, wolves were not frolicking companions for the Expedition. On their way back through North Dakota in July 1806, a small subparty separated from the main group and experienced wolves closer "at hand" than they would have preferred, as recorded by Clark on August 8: "On the night of the 26th . . . a Wolf bit Sergt. Pryor through his hand when asleep, and this animal was So vicious as to make an attempt to Seize Windsor, when Shannon fortunately Shot him. Sergt. Pryers hand was nearly recovered." The members of this small group were not having a particularly pleasant outing, as Indians had stolen all their horses earlier the same day. They were able to catch up with the rest of the Expedition by building two canoes from sapling frames over which they stretched buffalo hides, in the manner that they had learned from the Mandan Indians earlier.

The Expedition had ample opportunity to observe wolves in action. Sergeant Gass provided some insight into the hunting behavior of wolves on July 27, 1806:

> In a fine clear pleasant morning, myself and one of the men crossed the river with the horses, in order to go by land to the mouth of Maria's river: the rest of the party here are to go by water. We proceeded on through the plains about twenty miles, and in our way saw a great many buffaloe. We then struck Tansy or Rose river, [Teton River, Chouteau County, Montana] which we kept down about ten miles, and encamped. The land along this river is handsomely covered with Cotton wood timber and there is an abundance of game of different kinds. In our way we killed a buffaloe and a goat. [pronghorn antelope] The wolves in packs occasinally hunt these goats, which are too swift to be run down and taken by a single wolf. The wolves having fixed upon their intended prey and taken their stations, a part of the pack commence the chase, and running it in a circle, are at certain intervals relieved by others. In this manner they are able to run a goat down. At the falls where the wolves are plenty, I had an opportunity of seeing one of these hunts.

You have to really go out of your way to find a wolf today in the American West. But the situation is changing rapidly, most famously in Yellowstone National Park, but elsewhere as well (fig. 10.1). At a

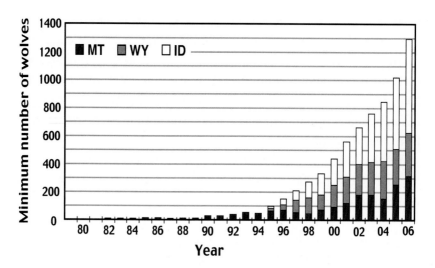

Fig. 10.1. Wolf population by state. U.S. Fish and Wildlife Service, "Rocky Mountain Wolf Recovery 2006 Annual Report."

time when most stories on environmental issues are full of doom and gloom, it is encouraging to find an example where things are going in the right direction.

The wolf was a symbol of wisdom, strength, and endurance to many Indian tribes. It was also seen as a great teacher of these virtues. The Indians were right. The wolf does indeed have a lot to teach us, and, fortunately, modern wildlife biologists and ecologists are paying close attention.

The showcase for wolf recovery is Yellowstone National Park. In 1995, the National Park Service and the U.S. Fish and Wildlife Service released fourteen wolves in the park. Wolves had been absent from the Yellowstone area since the early 1900s, having succumbed to government-sponsored hunting, trapping, and poisoning. The thinking of the time was that wolves had no redeeming qualities, since they killed livestock and game, especially elk that could other-

Fig. 10.2. An elk calf on the chief ranger's porch eating a Halloween pumpkin. Jim Peaco, National Park Service.

wise be turned into steak, barbecue, or hamburger. Get rid of wolves, and you should have a lot more elk to shoot or to stand around and look noble for the tourists in the national parks. It worked. The elk population exploded. Eventually, there were so many elk that the park became overrun with them.

All those elk had to eat something (fig. 10.2). As discussed in Chapter 4, cottonwood trees are a particularly rich food source, especially in the winter when there are few other dietary options. So the elk ate cottonwoods, along with aspen, willows, and other small deciduous trees and shrubs. They ate so many that young seedlings became scarce. The landscape of the Yellowstone area began to change in unpredicted and alarming ways as the normal streamside vegetation started to disappear.

By the 1960s, the Park Service resorted to trapping and shooting to try to limit the herd size to around 3,000. This was a partial success as far as keeping the numbers down, but it was a publicity nightmare for obvious reasons. The image of park rangers gunning down placid elk is not what most visitors have in mind when they think of a national park, nor is it what the rangers imagined would be in their job description. The next strategy, particularly popular in the 1970s, was to encourage hunting by the public. It is illegal to hunt within a national park, but once an elk sets foot across the park boundary, he or she is fair game—if you have a generous definition of fair. The Park Service worked with hunters and outfitters to make sure the elk arrived when and where expected for the convenience of hunters, some of whom had been waiting for long minutes in their idling pickup trucks for the chance to fill their freezer with elk steak. Even one leading local newspaper recognized that this was "not necessarily the epitome of the sport."[2] Eventually, the Park Service basically gave up and decided to let nature take its course. But nature was broken, and the herd size ballooned to 20,000. The park had been converted to a feedlot for elk.

Mature trees were safe from ravenous elk since their foliage was out of reach, but no young trees were coming in to replace them, a phenomenon that ecologists call recruitment. That takes a lot of elk munching, especially for aspen, which is clonal and sends up prodigious numbers of young trees each year from root sprouts. The

2. "Montana Hasn't Run Out of Elk Yet," *Missoula Missoulian*, January 18, 2004.

effects became obvious after a few decades. Careful measurements made in 2003 indicated that there had been almost no new cotton-wood trees established between 1940 and 2000 when the elk numbers were out of hand. Seedlings began to reappear only in 2001, when the elk numbers finally began to drop in response to wolves (figs. 10.3–10.6).

The eventual solution was to "fix" nature, that is, bring back the wolf, even though this met with extreme, sometimes violent, resistance from local ranchers and national hunting advocacy groups such as the National Rifle Association (NRA). The elk numbers have begun to swing back into balance, decreasing by about 6 percent annually from a high of more than 20,000 in 1994 to about 8,300 in

Fig. 10.3. Sled used to transport wolves to be released in Yellowstone National Park in 1995. Jim Peaco, National Park Service.

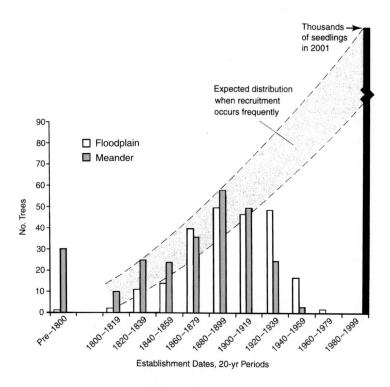

Fig. 10.4. Frequency distribution for establishment of narrow-leaf cotton-wood in the Lamar River Valley of Yellowstone National Park. The large number of seedlings in 2001 is a reflection of the reduction of elk numbers brought about by wolves. From Robert Beschta, "Cottonwoods, Elk, and Wolves in the Lamar Valley of Yellowstone National Park." Copyright 2003 Ecological Society of America.

Fig. 10.5. Comparison photographs taken in 1997 (*left*) and 2001 (*right*) illustrating recovery of streamside willows in Yellowstone National Park following wolf reintroduction that began in the winter of 1995–1996. From William J. Ripple and Robert L. Beschta, "Wolf Reintroduction, Predation Risk, and Cottonwood Recovery in Yellowstone National Park," 306. Copyright 2003 Elsevier Publishing.

Fig. 10.6. Captive wolf in Yellowstone National Park. Jim Peaco, National Park Service.

2004.[3] The wolves have settled in nicely and now number about 160 animals in a total of ten packs in the Yellowstone area. Each pack kills about one elk a day.[4]

Such developments have not been accepted calmly by the NRA, many of whose members are furious with the government "bureau-crats" who brought back the wolf. In 2004, the NRA-published magazine the *American Hunter* railed against the "idiocy of introduc-ing an indiscriminate killer among populations of carefully managed elk, deer, mountain sheep, moose and livestock." They cite "experts" who claim that "the ecosystem north of Yellowstone National Park has been, for all practical purposes, sterilized of wildlife."[5]

Feelings on the subject of wolf reintroduction run deep. Many ranchers are outspoken critics of the new wolf policy, since they (or rather their livestock) bear the direct consequences of errant wolf kills. In an effort to address the concerns of ranchers, the Defenders of Wildlife, a private conservation group, is compensating ranchers for losses that can be traced directly to wolves (table 10.1). Since the payments began in 1987, a total of more than $506,000 has been paid to 396 ranchers.

The absence of wolves also precipitated another serious problem—one that ecologists call mesopredator release. With the big-daddy predators, such as wolves, gone, the middle-size ones took over. "Meso" means middle(-size), of course, but it might be more ap-propriate to translate it as "measly." In Yellowstone and most of the West, this means primarily coyotes. In some situations, mesopreda-tors might include raccoons, foxes, opossums, or skunks, but it is usually the coyote that causes the worst ecosystem imbalance.

3. U.S. Department of the Interior, National Park Service, "Wolves of Yellow-stone," n.p.

4. See Jim Robbins, "Lessons from the Wolf."

5. Chuck Adams, "The Wolf Trap," 39.

Table 10.1. Tally of livestock killed from 1987 to 2004 by wolves and the compensation provided to ranchers by Defenders of Wildlife	
Greater Yellowstone ecosystem	**Southwest, Mexican wolves**
Cattle: 188	Cattle: 70
Sheep: 689	Sheep: 1
Other: 42	Other: 6
Total compensation: $247,866	Total compensation: $34,023
Central Idaho	**Northwest Montana**
Cattle: 134	Cattle: 129
Sheep: 554	Sheep: 89
Other: 4	Other: 7
Total compensation: $142,665	Total compensation: $78,649
Source: Defenders of Wildlife, "Northern Rockies Wolf Compensation Guidelines."	

When the Expedition hit the Great Plains, the coyote was essentially unknown to science. Paul Cutright suggests that Lewis should be credited with its discovery for modern science.[6] The fact that coyotes were unknown to science in 1805 is a good indication of just how little Euro-Americans really knew about the West. Although coyotes are one of the icons of the American West, they have definitely gotten out of hand in recent years. The coyote has prospered perhaps more than any other North American animal in the past two centuries. Their range has expanded at least 40 percent in the United States since the elimination of wolves.[7] They now can be found from Alaska to Florida.

6. Cutright, *Lewis and Clark*, 85.
7. See Andrea S. Laliberte and William J. Ripple, "Range Contractions of North American Carnivores and Ungulates," 126.

Just as with the elk, too much of a good thing can be harmful. Coyotes are very good at catching small rodents and rabbits—so good, in fact, that there are hardly any left over for owls, foxes, or any other predator, for that matter. Yellowstone of the 1990s was extremely coyote-rich but fox-poor. Biodiversity, a key feature of ecosystem health, thus took a double hit—that is, few rodents and few predators besides coyotes. Reduced diversity in any ecosystem is a clear sign that something serious is out of balance. Putting it back in balance was possible once the one missing piece (wolves) was put back in the equation.

The reappearance of wolves is also having a surprisingly positive effect on pronghorn numbers in Yellowstone. Pronghorn were once extremely abundant in the Yellowstone area, especially along river valleys. By the 1970s, even with the wolves long gone, the pronghorn numbers were down to fewer than 150. Despite Gass's observations on wolves hunting pronghorns, their success rate must have been low. Historically, wolves had little impact on pronghorn populations, as evidenced by the large number of pronghorn in pre-Euro-American times. A wolf is hard-pressed to sprint at thirty-five miles per hour, whereas a pronghorn can sustain bursts of sixty miles per hour for three to four minutes. Even young fawns, only a few hours old, can outrun a wolf. Pronghorn apparently evolved to outrace American cheetahs, now extinct (see Chapter 1 for extinction of megafauna), so outrunning a wolf is not a problem (fig. 10.7). It is no wonder that Clark wrote on September 17, 1804, that the motion of pronghorn "appeared reather the rappid flight of birds than the motion of quadrupeds."

Coyotes, on the other hand, are proficient at catching pronghorn fawns.[8] In areas where coyotes are abundant, the median age at death

---

8. See John A. Byers and D. W. Smith, "Wolves Improve Pronghorn Fawn Survival in Yellowstone National Park."

Fig. 10.7. North American cheetah pursuing a pronghorn in the Great Basin region in the Late Pleistocene. Lewis and Clark were about twelve thousand years too late to see such scenes. Courtesy of Michael Rothman Natural Science Illustration (http://www.michaelrothman.com).

of young pronghorn has been measured to be only six days, with only 3 percent of litters having one surviving fawn. However, 46 percent of litters had one survivor in the nearby Lamar Valley, where wolves have made a strong comeback. Wolves will not tolerate coyotes being in their territory, and the pronghorn have benefited from the wolves' belligerency. With the continued rebound of wolves, things are looking better for the pronghorn. When Lewis and Clark came through, there were perhaps 50 million pronghorn in the West. Within a century, that number was down to about 10,000. These numbers are now back up to perhaps 800,000, although this has little to do with wolves and more to do with wise conservation and the establishment of pronghorn reserves.[9] This is one of the more compelling success stories of modern wildlife management.

The reappearance of wolves also favorably impacts grizzly bears. Grizzly bears have been reduced to a nonfactor in most of the West, though a few (about 500, maybe less) have held out in Yellowstone and Glacier National parks.[10] Generally, there is less enthusiasm for reintroducing grizzlies into areas from which they have been extirpated because of the threat they pose to humans. However, the grizzlies in Yellowstone appear to be benefiting from wolf-killed elk leftovers. Bears rarely prey directly on elk, but wolves do, of course. Grizzlies come along later and take possession of the carcass. Large numbers of ravens, magpies, and eagles also benefit (fig. 10.8). As a recent article in *Scientific American* put it, "Wolves have also thrown the doors to the Yellowstone meat market wide open."[11]

Another major piece missing in the ecosystems of the West today is fire. As with wolves, grizzlies, and buffalo, fire was a common feature, more or less taken for granted by early Europeans. Fire was a major factor in maintaining the richness and fertility of the prairies of the Great Plains through which Lewis and Clark passed. Despite his limitations with respect to grammar and spelling, Clark rose admirably to the occasion to describe the beauty he encountered in eastern Kansas on July 4, 1804:

> one of the most butifull Plains, I ever Saw, open & butifully diversified with hills & vallies all presenting themselves to the river covered with grass and a few scattering trees a handsom Creek meandering thro. . . . The Plains of this countrey are covered with a Leek Green Grass, well calculated for the sweetest

9. Kemble S. Canon, "Management of Coyotes for Pronghorn?"
10. See David J. Mattson et al., "Grizzly Bears."
11. Robbins, "Lessons from the Wolf."

Fig. 10.8. Ravens and magpies sharing a wolf-killed elk in Yellowstone National Park. Jim Peaco, National Park Service.

and most norushing hay—interspersed with Cops [copses] of trees, Spreding their lofty branchs over Pools Springs or Brooks of fine water. Groops of Shrubs covered with the most delicious froot is to be seen in every direction, and nature appears to have exerted herself to butify the Senery by the variety of flours <raiseing> Delicately and highly flavered raised above the Grass, which Strikes & profumes the Sensation, and amuses the mind.

Lewis later, on September 16, 1804, emphasized the importance of fire in maintaining the prairies:

The country broken on the border of the river about a mile, when the level planes commence and extend as far as the eye can reach on either side; as usual no timber appeared except such as from the steep declivities of hills, or their moist situations, were sheltered from the effects of the fire. these extensive planes had been lately birnt and the grass had sprung up and was about three inches high. vast herds of Buffaloe deer Elk and Antilopes were seen feeding in every direction as far as the eye of the observer could reach.

Lewis further indicated his fundamental grasp of the factors at play in a letter he wrote to his mother, Lucy Marks, the following March while at Fort Mandan: "This want of timber is by no means attributeable to a deficiency in the soil to produce it, but ows it's orrigine to the ravages of the fires, which the natives kindle in these plains at all seasons of the year."[12]

The prairie benefits a number of ways from fire. Old, dead grass is removed, thus allowing for rapid growth of fresh, new grass. The nutrients (such as nitrogen and phosphorous) in the old grass are released to the soil where they become available for new growth. Last, fires prevent shrubs and trees from encroaching into the prairie. These benefits were well known to the Indians, who were responsible for setting many wildfires to provide better grazing for buffalo and to maintain an open landscape in which it was easier to travel and hunt.

The prairies, especially the spectacular tall-grass prairies of eastern Kansas, are essentially gone. It's not just fire that's missing. It is the whole darn ecosystem. And it just does not make much sense to think about reintroducing fire when the territory in question is an endless field of wheat or corn.

There are only a few small patches of native prairie left in the plains. The best examples are those managed by the Nature Conservancy in Kansas such as the Tallgrass Prairie National Preserve and the Konza Prairie Biological Station. These areas are carefully

12. Jackson, *Letters of the Expedition,* 223.

managed by scientists who understand the importance of fire—the "red buffalo." As a result, these reserves have been restored to something close to a natural setting, although of course the great herds of buffalo cannot be replicated. Also, the scale is limited compared to the original four hundred thousand square miles of tall-grass prairie that once covered the North American continent. In this regard, the situation is somewhat similar to the tiny fraction of old-growth forests that have been spared in the Pacific Northwest. The fragments that we have left of these ecosystems are sometimes referred to as living museums more than intact functional forces in nature.

The Indians of the Rocky Mountains also used wildfire as a management tool. Lewis and Clark reported several such Indian-set fires between Gates of the Mountains (near Helena, Montana) and Carmen Creek (near Salmon, Idaho) as they passed through in the late summer of 1805, as illustrated by the following journal excerpts: July 25 (Clark): "On the North Side the Indians have latterly Set the Praries on fire, the Cause I can't account for." August 4 (Lewis): "The Indians appear on some parts of the river to have distroyed a great proporiton of the little timber which there is by seting fire to the bottoms." August 31 (Clark): "The Countrey is Set on fire for the purpose of Collecting the different bands."

There is other evidence from modern scientific studies that Indians in the Rocky Mountains used fire to shape landscapes. For instance, large concentrations of airborne charcoal have been detected in bog sediments in western Montana, with the abundance of this charcoal greatly increasing in the past two thousand years when numerous Indians were in the area.[13] Fire-scarred trees are often observed to be more abundant in areas known to have been inhabited by Indians. Careful comparisons have revealed that the mean

13. Stephen W. Barrett and Stephen F. Arno, "Indian Fires as an Ecological Influence in the Northern Rockies."

fire interval (MFI), or the average interval between fires, was 9.1 years for the heavily used areas, as opposed to 18.2 years in remote areas where fires were predominantly caused by lightning. Using old fire scars and modern records, other studies have shown that the pre-1860 MFI interval was around 5.5 years, whereas the modern interval is 12.5 years.

Although Clark may have been puzzled by the reasons that Indians set fires, he probably came to a better understanding a few weeks later, on September 4, 1805, when struggling through the mountains of northern Idaho that he found to be "Steep & almost inaxcessible [with] much falling timber which fatigues our men & horses exceed-

Fig. 10.9. A stand of mixed conifers on the eastern slopes of the Oregon Cascade Range. The thick, crowded nature of such stands made them difficult to travel through and vulnerable to wildfire. Photo by the author.

ingly, in Slipping over So great a number of logs added to the Steep assents and decents of the Mounts."

Today, foresters refer to these choked forests as dog-hair stands (fig. 10.9). They are a particular feature of lodgepole pine (*Pinus contorta*) that tends to be fairly modest in stature anyway. The Indians wished to maintain a semiopen nature of the forests where they did most of their traveling and hunting. An open stand also promoted the growth of grasses and understory shrubs for the benefit of grazing and browsing by horses and deer.

Some forests, particularly the impressive stands of nearly pure ponderosa pine (*Pinus ponderosa*), found in moderately dry parts of the West from British Columbia to Arizona, were famous for their open nature due to frequent low-intensity ground fires that swept through the forest floor at intervals of 8 to 12 years and eliminated practically all brush and young trees, leaving only the large, widely spaced mature trees. By the time the first automobiles appeared in the West, it was still possible to drive for miles and miles through these stands without the need for any developed roads (fig. 10.10).

Throughout most of the 1900s, the policy in the American West was to aggressively suppress wildfires to the extent practical. Considering the tremendous potential for destruction, this policy certainly seems reasonable. It is also expensive. For 2002, a particularly bad year, fire suppression in the West cost $1.8 billion.[14] This is a great bargain in terms of lives, timber, and structures saved. But just as wolves are a vital part of western ecosystems, so is fire, and the total exclusion of fire has thrown nature out of balance.

Savvy firefighters have a saying that is particularly germane in this context: "You cannot really put out a forest fire. All you can do

14. Wildland Fire Leadership Council, "Large Fire Suppression Costs: Strategies for Cost Management," n.p.

Fig. 10.10. Ponderosa pine forest from central Oregon, ca. 1915. The lack
of understory was typical for vast areas where frequent though low-intensity
ground fires swept the forest floor clean on a regular basis. Oregon Historical
Society, no. Gi609.

is put it off." In other words, fire is inevitable. After a century of fire suppression, the forests have become thick with crowded and weakened trees and with vast accumulation of deadwood, that is, fuel. When fire comes, as it eventually must, the intensity and destruction can be awesome. Restoring balance will require the return of fire, an enlightened view that is now prevalent among ecologists, wildlife biologists, and land managers. As of 2005, the federal interagency policy is that "fire, as a critical natural process, will be integrated into land and resource management plans and activities on a landscape scale and across agency boundaries. Response to wildland fires is based on ecological, social and legal consequences of the fire."[15] This language is somewhat ambiguous and has been chosen carefully since the issue has become so political. The federal agencies appear to be backing off a bit from some of their earlier (2004) language that acknowledged that wildfire is "a critical natural process" that "must be reintroduced into the ecosystem . . . based on the best science available."[16]

Just as with wolves, Yellowstone National Park has proved to be the showcase for the reintroduction of fire, though the process has not been as planned or as deliberate as with wolves. The breaking point came in 1988, a particularly dry year when fires consumed 793,000 acres, about 36 percent of the park's total area, despite the frantic efforts of more than 25,000 firefighters and the expenditure of $120 million.[17] These fires had been put off about as long as possible. Although the immediate consequences in the park were distressing

15. National Fire and Aviation Executive Board Policy Directives Task Group, "Wildland Fire Use Implementation Procedures Reference Guide," n.p.

16. U.S. Forest Service, "Federal Wildland Fire Policy," accessed in 2004 at http://www.fs.fed.us/land/wdfire3.htm, but no longer available.

17. AllYellowstonePark.com, "History, Fire," n.p.

Fig. 10.11. Regeneration of lodgepole pine ten years after the fires of 1988 in Yellowstone National Park. Jim Peaco, National Park Service.

from a short-term human perspective, it soon became evident that recovery was occurring at a reassuring pace (fig. 10.11). Both the wildlife and the forests in Yellowstone are on track for a healthy long-term scenario—something that unfortunately cannot be said for many other regions of the West. At the heart of the issue is the need for us to understand that natural systems, such as forests and prairies, are not the equivalent of static museum display specimens. Conservation is not the same thing as preservation.

CHAPTER 11

Extra Pieces

As was their practice throughout the journey, the captains remarked about the general features of the landscape as they passed through the mountains and plains between the Rocky Mountains and the Cascade Range. Despite the general aridity of the West, it is clear that they were impressed with the beauty and richness of the land. For instance, on September 21, 1805, along the Clearwater River in Idaho, Clark noted, "The Countrey from the mountains to the river hills is a leavel rich butifull Pine Countrey badly watered, thinly timbered & covered with grass." Lewis remarked on similar country in eastern Washington on May 3, 1806, that "the land of the plains is much more fertile than below, less sand and covered with taller grass."

They were describing the sagebrush grasslands that are such a prominent feature east of the Cascade Range. The West has changed in many fundamental ways since Lewis and Clark passed through. Some are obvious, some not. Prairies have been converted to agriculture, wetlands drained, streams channelized and straightened, rivers dammed, bison replaced by cattle, and forests logged and converted into tree farms. But much that was great remains, especially on public lands such as those administered by the U.S. Forest Service, the Bureau of Land Management, and the National Park Service—lands that have not been "developed" or converted to agriculture, thus preserving a certain wildness. In Idaho, 70 percent of the land area is owned by the state or federal government.[1] Adjacent states are also faring well, with Oregon at 60 percent and Washington at 42 percent. Although these public lands are semipreserved and at least have the feel of being dominated by natural forces, there is sometimes a disturbing element of validity in designating the managing agencies as the Deforestation Service, the Bureau of Livestock and Mining, and the National Parking Lot Service, as the environmentalist writer Edward Abbey has suggested.

To the casual observer, the open range still looks pretty good: a lot of sagebrush and open sky, not much concrete or other signs of human presence. But to the trained eye, those signs are there big time. In particular, two powerful and intertwined forces of change—invasive plant species and wildfires—have radically altered the landscape throughout vast areas of the West on a scale that is difficult to fully comprehend. With respect to invasive plant species, two of the chief offenders are cheatgrass (*Bromus tectorum*) and spotted knapweed (*Centaurea maculosa*). There is no mention of either of these species in journals from the Expedition because the plants were not present. Nowadays, a traveler in much of the West would be hardpressed to be out of sight of either of these species.

Both of these species are native to Eurasia and were introduced into North America in the 1800s. It is difficult to trace their exact origin, but the best guess is that cheatgrass escaped after it was brought in

1. National Wilderness Institute, "State by State Government Land Ownership," n.p.

by researchers in Washington State looking for new grasses to make hay. Knapweed may have been a contaminant in alfalfa seed from Asia Minor.

It is hard to imagine a worse weed than cheatgrass. Even the name sounds bad. After its introduction it spread quickly by the trampling hooves of cows and as a contaminant in wheat field plantings so that by the 1930s it was the dominant grass over whole counties in the drier parts of the Pacific Northwest (that is, east of the Cascade Range). It now infests more than one hundred million acres in the western states, making it perhaps the most abundant invasive plant in the United States.[2] Aldo Leopold was one of the first and most eloquent writers to call attention to the cheatgrass problem:

> Today the honey-colored hills that flank the northwestern mountains derive their hue not from the rich and useful bunch-grass and wheatgrass which once covered them, but from the inferior cheat which has replaced these grasses. The motor-ist who exclaims about the flowing contours that lead his eye upward to far summits is unaware of this substitution. It does not occur to him that hills, too, cover ruined complexions with ecological face powder.[3]

The name "cheat" is well deserved, since the grass cheats farmers, ranchers, and wildlife from deriving the full benefit of the land by displacing native plants, reducing biodiversity and spreading fires. The economic costs arising from ecosystem damage, lost productivity, and control efforts range into the billions of dollars annually. There are so many problems with cheatgrass it is hard to know where to

2. R. N. Mack, "Invasion of *Bromus tectorum L.* into Western North America: An Ecological Chronicle."

3. Leopold, *A Sand County Almanac*, 155–56.

begin. Perhaps the most serious downside is that this grass replaces the more desirable native bunchgrasses. The bunchgrasses include species such as Idaho fescue (*Festuca idahoensis*) and bluebunch-wheatgrass (*Pseudoroegneria spicata,* previously *Agropyron spicatum*) that provide rich grazing for wildlife and livestock. The term *bunchgrass* is somewhat self-descriptive since these grasses consist of multiple-stem tight clusters of grasses. In contrast, cheatgrass is a spindly, usually one-stemmed annual that withers away in early summer.

Ecosystems dominated by bunchgrass and sagebrush have evolutionarily adapted to burn roughly every few decades. In the natural order of things, this was not a problem, since the fires were of low intensity and the bunchgrasses could easily resprout and even benefit from the release of nutrients brought about by the fire. But cheatgrass interrupts this natural cycle because it alters the fire pattern. Cheatgrass cheats the bunchgrass as well because it starts growing early in the season, depriving the natural grasses of the limited reserve of soil moisture. Cheatgrass matures and then dries out before the bunchgrasses have hardly gotten started. As the stems, leaves, and flowers of cheatgrass dry out, they become an ideal fuel for early-season fires that can burn the bunchgrasses before their seeds have had time to mature. Not only are these wildfires early in the season, but they are also more frequent, perhaps every three to five years. Put simply, "fire begets cheat grass and cheat grass begets fire."[4] Given enough time, the cheatgrass eventually displaces the native grasses.

This is really bad news for grazing animals. Cheatgrass is of low nutritional value compared to native bunchgrasses. Furthermore, the seeds (actually the fruits) are a real menace due to some wicked armature. The fruits are covered with stiff, barblike hairs that function

4. See R. Devine, "That Cheatin' Heartland."

Fig. 11.1. Cheatgrass in early fruit stage (A) and the later mature fruit stage showing the dry, spiny awns (B). Photos by Dr. Kimberlyn Williams, California State University–San Bernardino.

like a small and particularly bothersome porcupine quill (fig. 11.1). These miniquills pierce the insides of the animals' skin and mouth to create sores. The damage they do to eyes, nostrils, and intestines can be even worse. For some animals, such as domestic dogs, these quills can aggregate between their toe pads and burrow into the skin, creating disabling pain. As with the porcupine quill, the burrowing goes only one way and can even be fatal, since the fruit-darts continue to work their way inward, possibly ending up in the lungs or other vital areas. It is no coincidence that cowboys wear high boots without laces, since the cheatgrass makes any other arrangement impractical (fig. 11.2). Tennis shoes are a bad idea in cheatgrass country.

Fig. 11.2. Landscape from near Winnemucca, Nevada, that has been converted from sagebrush steppe to nearly pure cheatgrass due to fire intervals of fewer than ten years. Photo provided by Bridget Lair, U.S. Geological Survey.

Although cheatgrass was not yet around to pester Lewis and Clark, there was a native grass with similar pesky tendencies. Needle-and-thread grass (*Hesperostipa comata*), a common native of western grasslands, also has a spiky, barbed fruit that penetrates clothing and fur. This species was common on the Montana prairies, where Lewis described it on Friday, July 26, 1805:

> The high lands are thin meagre soil covered with dry low sedge and a species of grass also dry the seeds of which are armed with a long twisted hard beard at the upper extremity while the lower point is a sharp subulate firm point beset at it's base with little stiff bristles standing with their points in a contrary direction to the subulate point to which they answer as a barb and serve also to pres it forward when onece entered a small distance. these barbed seed penetrate our mockersons and leather legings and give us great pain untill they are removed. my poor dog suffers with them excessively, he is constantly binting and scratching himself as if in a rack of pain.

Needle-and-thread grass also resembles cheatgrass in that the barbed seed can injure the mouths of grazing animals in the summer. Unlike cheatgrass, however, needle-and-thread grass is a perennial bunchgrass and does have some redeeming qualities, such as its usefulness in stabilizing eroded or degraded sites. It is also a tolerable forage species early in the growing season before it dries out and toughens up (fig. 11.3).

Since cheatgrass is such a nasty customer, it is not surprising that science has turned its attention to the issue of control. The results are mixed and not encouraging. A large number of herbicides will kill it, but none are selective for cheatgrass only. Also, the cost of herbicides can be prohibitive, especially when applied to vast arid lands that support marginal economic return—that is, pretty much anywhere where cheatgrass is found in the West. Seeding, mowing,

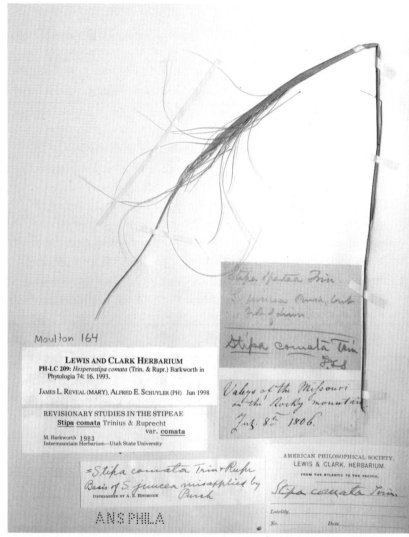

Fig. 11.3. Original herbarium specimen of needle-and-thread grass col-
lected by the Expedition. Pursh's notation, still attached, reads, "Valeys of the
Missouri in the Rocky mountains. July 8th 1806." Botany Department, the
Academy of Natural Sciences, Philadelphia.

or controlled burning before seeds mature can work somewhat, but again the problem is one of scale and costs. There is simply no current method of control that is sufficiently powerful and efficient to be of much consequence outside of small, intense, and expensive efforts.

Despite the gloom surrounding cheatgrass, there is some cause for hope of control with the use of biological agents, particularly certain types of bacteria of the genus *Pseudomonas*. Bacteria of this genus are frequently found in soil, water, and vegetation. Some of the pseudomonads are a cause of several problematic diseases in crop plants. A few others can be opportunistic pathogens in animals. These bacteria are so common, even in healthy plants, that they can often be detected in numbers in excess of ten million per gram of plant tissue without any apparent harm. Plants have an ambivalent relationship with these bacteria—sometimes pathogenic, sometimes beneficial, and most often more or less neutral.

This is a complicated story that keeps many soil and plant microbiologists productively occupied. The beneficial effects have been attributed to at least four possible factors in which the bacteria may (1) produce chemicals that inhibit pathogens or other plants, (2) produce phytohormones that stimulate plant growth, (3) produce chemicals that assist the plant in taking up iron from the soil, or (4) capture ("fix") nitrogen from the air and make it available to the plant host.

Several species of root-inhabiting pseudomonads produce a chemical (phenazine-1-carboxylic acid) that inhibits cheatgrass. This compound is most effective during the early stages of growth when it suppresses germination and root elongation of cheatgrass. Native grasses are much less sensitive. Since cheatgrass is an annual, it depends on resprouting from new seeds every year. Reducing the percentage of germination over several years may shift the competitive edge away from cheatgrass and back to native bunchgrasses.

Under laboratory conditions, this compound can inhibit root growth by 99 percent.[5]

These same bacteria have one other big thing going for them: they inhibit pathogenic fungi of wheat, particularly a fungus called *Gaeumannomyces graminis* var. *tritici* that causes a serious disease called "take-all." Thus, the bacteria could do double duty in wheat fields by suppressing both cheatgrass and pathogenic fungi. This is an area of active research that may someday provide considerable benefits, especially if strains of bacteria can be obtained that are powerful enough and persistent in the environment. One possible route to this goal is through the use of genetic engineering to produce superstrains of bacteria. Release of genetically engineered microorganisms into the field is, of course, controversial, but it might be worth it in this case if the ecological scourge of cheatgrass can be controlled.

Cheatgrass has a coconspirator equally bent on ecological rampage in the West in the form of knapweeds such as spotted knapweed (*Centaurea maculosa*), diffuse knapweed (*Centaurea diffusa*), Russian knapweed (*Centaurea repens*), and yellow starthistle (*Centaurea solstitialis*) (fig. 11.4). Knapweed has a different set of evil tricks that has allowed it to take over large portions of sagebrush habitat (fig. 11.5). Knapweed is a specialist in chemical warfare. It contains a bitter, toxic compound called cnicin that discourages grazing. Up to 4 percent of the leaf dry weight can be cnicin.[6] It tastes nasty, even to a cow. The cnicin even has antimicrobial properties that can interfere with microbial action in the rumen that is necessary for digestion. As if that were not enough, knapweed contains a second chemical

5. See David R. Gealy, S. Gurusiddaiah, and Alex G. Ogg Jr., "Isolation and Characterization of Metabolites from *Pseudomonas syringae*–Strain 3366 and Their Phytotoxicity against Certain Weed and Crop Species."

6. See Bret E. Olson and Rick G. Kelsey, "Effect of *Centaurea maculosa* on Sheep Rumen Microbial Activity and Mass in Vitro."

Fig. 11.4. Diffuse knapweed (*Centaurea diffusa*) from near The Dalles, Oregon. Copyright 2007 Mark Turner.

Fig. 11.5. Heavy infestation of spotted knapweed in the Bitterroot Valley of western Montana. Photo by Jim Story, Montana State University.

(catechin) that inhibits neighboring desirable plants such as native bunchgrasses. Few animals will eat knapweed, and few other plants can stand up to its noxious chemicals. Knapweed is even fairly indifferent to fires. It may get singed but will often just resprout. Even if the plant is killed, the large number of tiny seeds in the soil will likely result in an eventual increase in knapweed following fire. Like cheatgrass, it has a perverse preference for overgrazed land where the disturbed soil provides an ideal site for seed germination. Also like cheatgrass, knapweed is difficult to control. Herbicides work, but they are expensive and nonselective.

Knapweed's use of catechin to inhibit neighboring plants is a classic case of allelopathy—the term used for the process by which some plants gain a competitive advantage by producing chemicals that adversely affect other plants. Literally, the word *allelopathy* means "making others sick." If you are a plant and your neighbor is crowding you out, you can dump toxins on them to make them sick, thereby leaving more resources (moisture, light, nutrients, and so on) for you. The ecological literature is full of descriptions and explanations of allelopathy, but it has been extremely difficult until recently to provide unequivocal evidence that allelopathy is a legitimate phenomenon. Knapweed, with the assistance of modern molecular biology, has provided a ironclad case for allelopathy that should convince even the most skeptical doubter. Although this discovery may have resolved a long-term academic debate, the real-world ecological implications are far from academic. Simply put, knapweed is about as bad as invasive plants get.

Spotted knapweed leaks catechin into the soil in substantial amounts, up to 400 micrograms per gram of soil.[7] At that concentration, there is almost 1 full gram in 5 pounds of soil. An acre of infested ground would contain more than 700 pounds of catechin![8] Catechin has strong herbicidal properties. It even compares fairly well with 2,4-D, the most commonly used synthetic herbicide in the world and the active ingredient for the infamous weed killer Agent Orange that the U.S. military used in Vietnam. You need only about a tenfold higher concentration of catechin than 2,4-D to get the job done.[9]

7. See Harsh P. Bais et al., "Allelopathy and Exotic Plant Invasion: From Molecules and Genes to Species Interactions."

8. Assuming an average weight for soil of 2 million pounds per acre to a depth of 7 inches. These are values often used by soil scientists and provide only a rough calculation, but are still useful as a best guess for an upper limit.

9. Harsh P. Bais et al., "Enantiomeric-Dependent Phytotoxic and Antimicrobial Activity of (±)-Catechin: A Rhizosecreted Racemic Mixture from Spotted Knapweed."

What would happen if you applied 2,4-D at the rate of 70 pounds per acre, a rate at least thirty-five times the norm? Every single green plant would wither and die. The soil microflora would practically disappear. The ground would become a sterile wasteland. The rest of us would hope some responsible government agency will come and lock you up for incredible stupidity. These numbers may be a little soft, but it is clear that knapweed does not fool around. When it moves into the neighborhood, almost every other plant moves out—except, that is, for other spotted knapweed plants. They are immune to their own toxin.

For a typical response to catechin, consider the cases of native North American grasses such as Idaho fescue (*Festuca idahoensis*, from sagebrush communities) and Junegrass (*Koeleria micrantha*, a prairie grass). When catechin was added to soil in which these grasses were growing, seed germination was almost completely inhibited and the few plants that did grow were much smaller (fig. 11.6).[10]

Catechin causes a "wave of cell death" in tender young roots that can be seen under the microscope within minutes following application. There is an even quicker wave of damaging reactive oxygen species (such as hydrogen peroxide and superoxide) that moves up the root, indicating a biochemical shock response to stress. Root hairs, the tiny nutrient-absorbing fluff on the outer surface of roots, pop open and spill out their contents. All of these responses have been documented on some spectacular movies and can be seen at http://www.sciencemag.org/cgi/content/full/301/5638/1377/DC1. Within one hour after catechin treatment, 956 different genes of the treated plants show higher activity (actually "expression") in an attempt to respond to the chemical attack, thus indicating a massive, systemwide response. It is not enough.

10. Ibid.

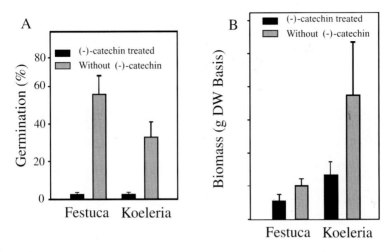

Fig. 11.6. The effects of catechin addition on the germination (A) and biomass (B) of two species of native North American grasses growing in natural field soil in pots. From Bais et al., "Allelopathy and Exotic Plan Invasion," 1378. Reprinted with permission of the American Association for the Advancement of Science.

As with cheatgrass, it is extremely difficult to control knapweed. The simplest and often most effective means is hand pulling. This can clean up small areas and prevent its spread in critical areas such as along highway corridors. State highway departments sometimes will send out knapweed patrols for this purpose. But the amount of land subject to hand control is minuscule compared to the huge areas of land, especially public land, where heavy grazing has created conditions in which knapweed proliferates. Many state departments of agriculture as well as federal agencies have active programs to control knapweed that feature publicity campaigns to help the public (ranchers in particular) recognize their enemy (fig. 11.7).

Unlike the case with cheatgrass, it looks now as though biocontrol of knapweed is not only possible but actually working in many areas. Entomologists have imported a range of flies, weevils, and beetles

Fig. 11.7. "Wanted" poster for spotted knapweed. Shelly Fischman, Bureau of Land Management.

Fig. 11.8. Knapweed seedhead fly (*Urophora quadrifasciata*). Adult on knapweed flower (A) and larva in seedhead (B). Credits: A, Robert D. Richard, USDA, APHIS, PPQ, http://www.forestryimages.org; B: University of Idaho Archives, University of Idaho, http://www.forestryimages.org.

that attack various species of knapweed in multiple ways. Some of these insects mine the roots. Others feed in developing seed heads or munch on leaves or flowers. By 1998, thirteen knapweed biocontrol agents had been released in seventeen states. Populations of most of these are now self-maintaining and increasing rapidly.[11]

A good example can be found in the case of the seed-head gall flies (*Urophora affinis* and *U. quadrifasciata*), two species that are native to Eurasia (fig. 11.8). They were one of the first knapweed biocontrol agents introduced in the West and are now so common that they are considered nearly universally present wherever knapweed is found. Eggs laid in the flowers develop into gall-forming larvae that divert key nutrients away from developing seeds. Seed production can be reduced by up to 95 percent. The Oregon Department of Agriculture estimates that these biocontrol agents have the poten-

11. Ronald F. Lang et al., "Release and Establishment of Diffuse and Spotted Knapweed Biocontrol Agents by USDA, APHIS, PPQ, in the United States."

tial to reduce infestation by 50 percent within twenty years.[12] That certainly is promising, but as is so often the case in ecology, every manipulation by humans leads to unexpected ripple effects in the net of life. In this case, the increase in the number of gall flies is a boon for deer mice (*Peromyscus maniculatus*) who find the grubs an attractive food source.[13] These mice are reservoir hosts for a wide range of problematic human pathogens, including hantavirus, Lyme disease, and even plague. The control of knapweed may come with a high price with respect to the health of humans and wildlife.

12. Oregon Department of Agriculture, "Economic Analysis of Containment Programs, Damages, and Production Losses from Noxious Weeds in Oregon," n.p.

13. See Dean E. Pearson and Ragan M. Callaway, "Biological Control Agents Elevate Hantavirus by Subsidizing Deer Mouse Populations."

CHAPTER 12

———————— ⟨❧⟩ ————————

Climate Change and the Future of the American West

I n compliance with Jefferson's instructions, the captains made careful records of the weather. The entry for each day usually begins with a description of the conditions—for example, "a violent hard rain about day light this morning" (Clark, August 20, 1806) or "the morning was fair and the plains looked be-atifull" (Lewis, July 11, 1806). Prior to accidentally breaking all three of their mercury thermometers before crossing the Rocky Mountains, they were diligent in recording daily temperatures at sunrise and four in the afternoon. Likewise, they made careful notes of the "State of the weather" and "Course of the wind" twice daily.

Recent analysis of weather records has revealed that the Expedition experienced a fortuitous window of favorable climatic conditions. Certainly, they suffered from the stinging cold of a North Dakota winter and the unrelenting sogginess of a winter on the Northwest coast, but things could have been a lot worse. Throughout their route, the period between 1804 and 1806 was unusually cool and wet.[1] Thus they avoided drought conditions, such as the pronounced droughts of 1800 and 1808 that would have greatly impeded their river travel and reduced forage for game and horses. Had the weather been less cooperative, the Expedition could well have failed or been delayed for a year.

Much has changed in the American West since Lewis and Clark came through. Even more drastic changes are in store for the future. What is particularly troublesome about these future developments is that we are not just altering the landscape, removing or adding pieces of ecosystems. Instead, we are unintentionally altering the underlying support system—namely, the climate. For anyone interested in how nature works (and we all should be), this is cause for concern.

Climate change is such a hot issue in the news these days that it is easy to overlook the fact that it is already here. Despite the deliberate obfuscation of politicians, the science behind the causes of global warming is clear and easily agreed upon by almost all reputable climate scientists. In 1803, the concentration of CO_2 in the atmosphere was around 270 parts per million. In 2005, it is about 370 parts per million. The laws of physics are quite clear and indeed have been so since the Swedish chemist and Nobel prizewinner Svante August Arrhenius pointed out more than one hundred years ago that increased CO_2 in the atmosphere will inevitably trap more heat and cause global warming. This will have profound effects on natural systems in the West.

Let's begin by a brief look at the numbers relating to climate change in the Pacific Northwest. How has the climate changed, and how great will the future changes be? Regionwide, there has been a

---

1. Knapp, "Window of Opportunity."

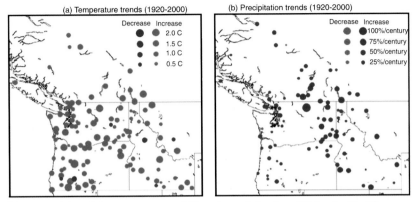

Fig. 12.1. Trends in temperature (A) and precipitation (B) in the Pacific Northwest from 1920 to 2000. From JISAO/SMA Climate Impacts Group, http://cses.washington.edu/cig/pnwc/cc.shtml.

warming of about 1.5°F since 1920 (fig. 12.1).[2] The warming has been fairly uniform and widespread. At a number of locations, the warming has actually been greater than 3.5°F. Over this same time period, the precipitation has increased around 22 percent on average, even greater in some areas such as eastern Washington, where the increase has been around 60 percent. These trends are expected to continue such that by 2040, the average annual temperature will have increased by 4.1°F. The models are inconclusive with respect to changes in precipitation, but most likely winters will be wetter.

Similar changes are in store for the rest of the West as well. For instance, the wonderfully productive cornfields of Iowa are going to find themselves in a climate roughly equivalent to that of present-day Mississippi, a situation they are surely poorly adapted for. The extent

2. P. Mote et al., "Impacts of Climate Variability and Change in the Pacific Northwest."

of the changes that are in store for the Iowa climate during this coming century is that alarming. By the end of the twenty-first century, temperatures across the plains are expected to rise 5–14°F in the summer and 9–22°F in the winter.[3] Winter precipitation will likely increase by about 30 percent, whereas summer rainfall may decline 10 to 35 percent. Even more troublesome, the rain that does come in the summer will be more likely to come in intense downpours that quickly run off, so drier soils and droughts seem inevitable.

Predicting the consequences of these coming changes is one of the most pressing issues in modern biology. Even if we had the political will to avert the coming changes, it is doubtful we could do much more than slow things down slightly. The forces at play are too great for us to do much more than ride them out, especially considering the attitude of the current administration in which government scientists are instructed to avoid using the term *climate change* in any official context and to instead talk about *climate variability* so as to enforce the false notion that we do not really know what is coming.

So what exactly is in store for nature and agriculture in the American West a century or so down the road? Part of the difficulty in answering this question is that even the best minds and supercomputers in the world cannot accurately predict the extent of the changes. The Pacific Northwest is particularly complex, since there already exists tremendous variation in climate, topography, and ecosystems within very short distances. Within distances of about one hundred miles, precipitation varies from fewer than eight inches per year to more than two hundred inches, winter lows from seldom below 60°F to frequent subzero temperatures, and elevation from sea level to more than fourteen thousand feet. Just describing the existing patterns of vegetation is a serious challenge.

3. Union of Concerned Scientists, "Climate Change in the Hawkeye State," n.p.

Just as the climate of Iowa appears to be changing to match that of present-day Mississippi, the climates in the Pacific Northwest are expected to shift perhaps three hundred miles northward or three thousand feet upward in elevation.[4] Many, if not most, major vegetation types will find themselves seriously misplaced. Over time, plant and animal communities can migrate and relocate to find a local climate to which they are adapted, but the normal time scale for these adjustments is far beyond what is being imposed on them by the sudden rush of human-induced climate change. How long does it take for a one thousand–year-old Douglas-fir forest to pull up stakes and move three hundred miles north? This is a troublesome question, of course, that becomes even more so when you ask: and what will be the *new* climate by the time the forest species manages to relocate?

If one assumes that the forests can migrate, there would be some major reallocation of the proportion of landscapes occupied by various vegetation types. For instance, on the eastern slopes of the Oregon Cascade Range, forested areas would decrease from 58 percent of the total area to about 12 percent due to the expansion of drought-tolerant juniper and sagebrush (fig. 12.2). On the western slopes of the Cascade Range, the commercially valuable western hemlock zone might decline from a current value of 56 percent to somewhere between 24 to 38 percent of the landscape (fig. 12.3). The alpine and cold-snow zones would literally be squeezed off the top of the mountains to the detriment of species such as Clark's nutcracker and whitebark pine (see Chapter 7). Furthermore, the new climate will favor an increase in disturbances, such as wildfires, storms, and outbreaks of insects and pathogens. Although these are already major

4. See Jerry F. Franklin et al., "Effects of Global Climate Change on Forests in Northwestern North America."

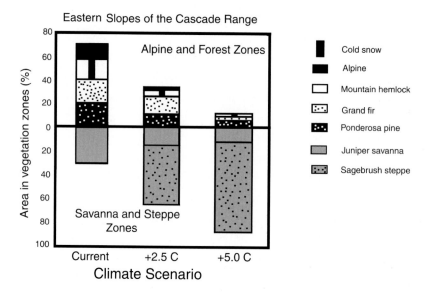

Fig. 12.2. Percentage of area of major vegetation types on the eastern slopes of the central Oregon Cascade Range under current climate and two likely future scenarios. From Franklin et al., "Effects of Global Climate Change," 239.

features of Northwest forests, their severity and frequency will likely increase, with catastrophic effects on huge areas.

Elsewhere in the West, the changes will be equally profound, though each subregion will have its own quirks and adjustments, some major, some not. One of the ways of describing the capacity for photosynthesis of forests is that of the Leaf Area Index (LAI). This is defined as the number of equivalent layers of leaves relative to any given unit of ground area, that is, the average leaf surface area (in square meters) that lies directly above one square meter of forest floor. Another way to think of LAI is to imagine yourself lying flat on your back on the forest floor while you shoot a rifle straight up. The number of times your bullet intercepts a leaf on its upward path equals the LAI. LAI values vary widely but are generally in

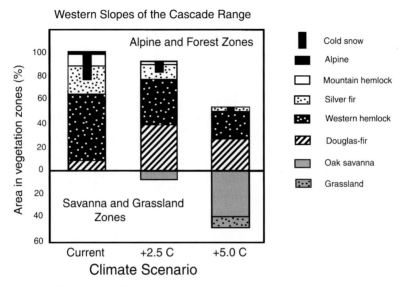

Fig. 12.3. Percentage of area of major vegetation types on the western slopes of the central Oregon Cascade Range under current climate and two likely future scenarios. From Franklin et al., "Effects of Global Climate Change," 238.

the range of three to ten for temperate evergreen forests and four to eight for temperate deciduous forests. Due to the extreme variation in existing climatic conditions, the LAI values in the West cover a wide range (fig. 12.4). A measure of LAI is a good indication of just how productive that particular forest, prairie, or cornfield is.

With the coming changes in climate, the LAI values in most of the West are likely to undergo substantial changes and with them the productivity of the landscapes and the well-being of all its inhabitants, human or not. It is not possible to accurately predict the magnitude of these changes, or even whether the changes will be positive or negative, but two reasonable scenarios are given in figure 12.5. The LAI may actually increase if one assumes a very modest temperature increase of 2.8°C (the UKMO model), or, alternatively, the LAI

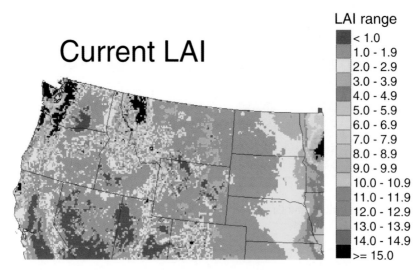

Fig. 12.4. Current Leaf Area Index values for the northwestern United States. From Bachelet et al., "Climate Change Effects." With kind permission of Ronald Neilson and Springer Science and Business Media, copyright 2001.

values may sharply decline if a temperature increase of 6.6°C (the HADCM2SUL model) is used in setting the model parameters.[5] Even though scientists cannot be confident of the scope of the changes in LAI values, there is general agreement that these ecosystems are in for a severe jolt of some kind. Some scientists are hoping that the negative effects can be somewhat offset by the so-called carbon-fertilization effect. The reasoning goes something like this: Plants need CO_2 in order to photosynthesize. As the concentration of CO_2 increases, this will enhance photosynthesis, thus making plants more productive. Although this is a valid phenomenon, there is a lot of

5. See Dominique Bachelet et al., "Climate Change Effects on Vegetation Distribution and Carbon Budget in the United States."

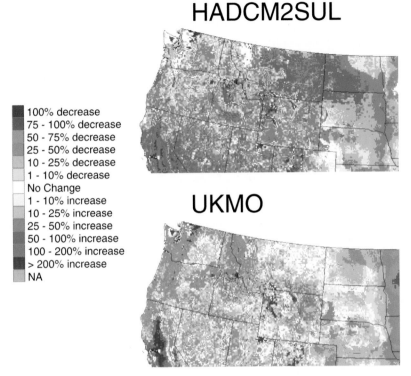

Fig. 12.5. Predicted changes in Leaf Area Index for the northwestern United States as a consequence of climate change as forecast by two different models. From Bachelet et al., "Climate Change Effects." With kind permission of Ronald Neilson and Springer Science and Business Media, copyright 2001.

uncertainty as to exactly how significant it will be in reality. Most ecologists expect the negative impacts of the altered climate to far outweigh any direct benefit from CO_2 fertilization. More wishful thinking can be used to imagine a scenario in which plants might adjust to their new climates by becoming increasingly efficient in their water use. The logic here is that what with all that extra CO_2 around, the stomata (leaf pores) will not need to be open as much in order to let CO_2 into the leaf. With the stomata more closed, there should be less loss of water vapor through transpiration, thus once again making the plants more productive. This sounds fine in theory, but the evidence so far indicates that trees do not actually increase their water-use efficiency in response to elevated CO_2.

These types of experiments are extremely difficult and expensive to conduct. Imagine growing a forest under conditions in which the CO_2 concentration is artificially altered while everything else (for example, temperature, light, humidity, and so on) remains the same, and then compare the growth of that forest to a control plot in which the CO_2 concentration remains at ambient levels. And do that with enough replicates to make it statistically meaningful. Such studies have been conducted on a limited scale, but not in intact forests in the American West. About the closest we can come is to look at experiments with a pine forest in North Carolina.[6] Train-car loads of compressed CO_2 were brought into the forest where the gas was carefully released from tall towers arranged in a thirty-meter-diameter ring. The CO_2 concentration in the air was monitored twenty-four hours a day with frequent releases of extra CO_2 so that the test plots maintained a CO_2 concentration that was 200 ppm higher than ambient (ambient = 360 ppm compared to 560 ppm in the test plots). Photosynthesis was in fact stimulated 50 to 60 percent by elevated CO_2, but there was no change in water savings. What this actually portends for forests is pretty much anyone's guess, but we are about to find out, and chances are we are not going to like the outcome. When you consider the negative consequences of an altered climate and the inability of the trees to increase their water-use efficiency, then most likely any direct benefit due to stimulation of photosynthesis is going to be of little consequence.

6. D. S. Ellsworth, "CO_2 Enrichment in a Maturing Pine Forest: Are CO_2 Exchange and Water Status in the Canopy Affected?"

CONCLUDING REMARKS

⟨ornament⟩

The Lewis and Clark Expedition was exceptionally successful from a number of perspectives, not the least of which was natural history. The early 1800s were a rich and productive time for natural history explorations. So much of the natural world was yet unknown to Western science. Vast areas of land were unexplored, especially in the Americas, Africa, and the South Pacific. New species of birds, mammals, and plants could be found just over the horizon or around the next bend of the river. Nowhere was the knowledge vacuum more complete than in the inland American West. Even the coyote was unknown to Euro-Americans prior to Lewis's discovery. According to Paul Cutright's generous count, the Expedition documented 185 species (or subspecies) of plants and animals that were new to science.[1] Modern taxonomists, less generous than Cutright, have whittled this number down, but the fact remains that Lewis and Clark discovered an impressive number of new species across a broad taxonomic spectrum. The captains have also justly been called "the writingest explorers of their time."[2] They

1. Paul A. Johnsgard, introduction to *Lewis and Clark,* by Cutright, x.
2. Jackson, *Letters of the Expedition,* v.

225

provided a wealth of new information about the distribution, life history, and importance to Indians of countless other species that were only scantily known previously. These accomplishments are even more remarkable considering that the captains were not professional naturalists or scientists. What they did have were keen minds and powers of observation, as well as an uncanny ability to insert themselves intimately into their surroundings and to understand how nature was operating around them.

The captains left a rich biological legacy that still speaks to us today. In testimony to Lewis and Clark's prowess as naturalists, the key features that caught their notice are still the center of attention to those with an eye toward nature and its workings: salmon, wolves, grizzlies, sagebrush, giant old-growth trees, prairies, elk, cottonwood, fossils, cat's ear lily, bitterroot, and camas.

Far beyond a great adventure story and a cataloging of new species, the Expedition has also provided us with some universal and enduring truths that transcend the examples discussed in this book. First and foremost is that the American West is still incredibly rich in natural resources and beauty. We should appreciate it, just as Lewis and Clark did. They had the benefit of extra excitement that comes with first discovery, but that does not mean we cannot feel the same wonder and awe.

Putting aside aesthetic or spiritual considerations, the American West also has scientific treasures. There are regrettably few places in the modern world where nature still works more or less intact and in proximity to an affluent and scientifically competent population. Of course, this is not universally true of the West, but it is true enough. We have great natural laboratories close at hand, including the greatest temperate rain forests in the world, deserts, mountains, prairies, and great rivers all crammed into a small corner of the world with great biological, geological, and climatic diversity. We also have good universities and colleges and trained scientists with the right disposition to poke under rocks and bushes to see what's out there. This book is largely their story.

The long-term history of nature in the American West is one of cycles of boom and bust. Go back long enough, and we would have found the landscape filled with horses, camels, mammoths, and a remarkable diversity of giant ground sloths. Humans wiped the slate clean ten thousand years ago, as we learned in Chapter 1. Huge numbers of bison, elk, grizzlies, and wolves moved in to fill the void. We wiped the slate clean again. Now what? The "slate" seems to be filled with cattle, wheat, and cheatgrass. Much of it will probably stay that way, but not all of it. There is still a lot of the Wild West left. Consider the words of the late Stephen Ambrose, noted historian and Lewis and Clark scholar, when asked what he considered noteworthy about the landscapes left behind: "I would say their vacancy. . . . I see it as an opportunity to challenge our generation. . . . [S]o long as we still have wild land intact, there will always be hope that the native plants and animals known to Lewis and Clark can be restored."[3] The lessons of Lewis and Clark are not lost, but rather can be used to guide us toward just such a goal.

3. Quoted in T. Wilkinson, "Rediscovering Lewis and Clark's America."

BIBLIOGRAPHY

Academy of Natural Sciences. "Harlan's Musk Ox (*Bootherium bombifrons*)." http://www.ansp.org/museum/jefferson/other-Fossils/bootherium.php.

Adams, Chuck. "The Wolf Trap." *American Hunter* 32 (2004): 37–43.

AllYellowstonePark.com. "History, Fire." http://www.yellowstone parknet.com/history/fires.php.

Alroy, John. "A Multispecies Overkill Simulation of the End-Pleistocene Megafaunal Mass Extinction." *Science* 292 (2001): 1893–96.

Ambrose, Stephen. *Undaunted Courage: Meriwether Lewis, Thomas Jefferson, and the Opening of the American West.* New York: Simon and Schuster, 1996.

American Forests. "National Register of Big Trees." http://www.americanforests.org/resources/bigtrees.

Bachelet, Dominique, Ronald P. Neilson, James M. Lenihan, and Raymond J. Drapek. "Climate Change Effects on Vegetation Distribution and Carbon Budget in the United States." *Ecosystems* 4 (2001): 164–85.

Bais, Harsh P., Ramarao Vepachedu, Simon Gilroy, Ragan M. Callaway, and Jorge M. Vivanco. "Allelopathy and Exotic Plant Invasion: From Molecules and Genes to Species Interactions." *Science* 301 (2003): 1377–80.

Bais, Harsh P., Travis S. Walker, Frank R. Stermitz, Ruth A. Hufbauer, and Jorge M. Vivanco. "Enantiomeric-Dependent Phytotoxic and Antimicrobial Activity of (±)-Catechin: A Rhizosecreted Racemic Mixture from Spotted Knapweed." *Plant Physiology* 128 (2002): 1173–79.

Barlow, Connie. *The Ghosts of Evolution: Nonsensical Fruit, Missing Partners, and Other Ecological Anachronisms.* New York: Basic Books, 2000.

Barot, S., M. Heino, L. O'Brien, and U. Dieckmann. "Long-Term Trend in the Maturation Reaction Norm of Two Cod Stocks." *Ecological Monographs* 14 (2004): 1257–71.

Barrett, Stephen W., and Stephen F. Arno. "Indian Fires as an Ecological Influence in the Northern Rockies." *Journal of Forestry* 80 (1982): 647–51.

Beschta, Robert L. "Cottonwoods, Elk, and Wolves in the Lamar Valley of Yellowstone National Park." *Ecological Applications* 13 (2003): 1295–309.

Bradshaw, H. D., and Douglas W. Schemske. "Allele Substitution at a Flower Color Locus Produces a Pollinator Shift in Monkeyflowers." *Nature* 426 (2003): 176–78.

Brown, P. T., M. J. Sutkna, R. P. Morwood, J. Soejono, E. Wayhu Saptomo, and Rokus Awe Due. "A New Small-Bodied Hominid from the Late Pleistocene of Flores, Indonesia." *Nature* 431 (2004): 1055–61.

Burness, Gary P., Jared Diamond, and Timothy Flannery. "Dinosaurs, Dragons, and Dwarfs: The Evolution of Maximal Body Size." *Proceedings of the National Academy of Sciences of the United States of America* 98 (2001): 14518–23.

Buttkus, Hans A., Robert J. Bose, and Duncan A. Shearer. "Terpenes in Essential Oil of Sagebrush (*Artemisia tridentata*)." *Journal of Agricultural and Food Chemistry* 25 (1977): 288–91.

Byers, John A., and D. W. Smith. "Wolves Improve Pronghorn Fawn Survival in Yellowstone National Park." International Wolf Center, 2004. http://www.wolf.org/wolves/index.asp.

Callahan, Frank. "The Genus *Calochortus*." In *Bulbs of North America*, ed. Jane McGary, 101–38. Portland: Timber Press, 2001.

Canon, S. Kemble. "Management of Coyotes for Pronghorn?" Texas Natural Resource Server, 1995. http://texnat.tamu.edu/symposia/coyote/p21.htm.

Carder, Al. *Forest Giants of the World, Past and Present.* Markham, Ontario: Fitzhenry and Whiteside, 1995.

Carson, Rachel. *Silent Spring.* Boston: Houghton Mifflin, 1962.

Cutright, Paul. *Lewis and Clark: Pioneering Naturalists.* 2d ed. Lincoln: University of Nebraska Press, 2003.

Davidson, A. *The Oxford Companion to Food.* Oxford: Oxford University Press, 1999.

Defenders of Wildlife. "Northern Rockies Wolf Compensation Guidelines." http://www.defenders.org/wolfcompguidelines.html.

Devine, Robert. "That Cheatin' Heartland." In *Alien Invasion: America's Battle with Non-native Animals and Plants,* ed. Robert Devine, 51–71. Washington, D.C.: National Geographic Society, 1998.

Douglas, David. *Journal Kept by David Douglas during His Travels in North America, 1823–1827.* New York: Antiquarian Press, 1959.

Earle, A. Scott, and James L. Reveal. *Lewis and Clark's Green World: The Expedition and Its Plants.* Helena, Mont.: Farcountry Press, 2003.

Eliott, Roy C. *The Genus* Lewisia. Worcestershire, England: Alpine Garden Society Bulletin, 1966.

Ellsworth, D. S. "CO$_2$ Enrichment in a Maturing Pine Forest: Are CO$_2$ Exchange and Water Status in the Canopy Effected?" *Plant, Cell, and Environment* 22 (1999): 461–72.

Everhart, Mike. "Oceans of Kansas Paleontology: Fossils from the Late Cretaceous Western Interior Sea." http://www.oceansof kansas.com.

Falkowski, Paul G., Miriam E. Katz, Allen J. Milligan, Katja Fennel, Benjamin S. Cramer, Marie Pierre Aubry, Robert A. Berner, Michael J. Novacek, and Warren M. Zapol. "The Risk of Oxygen over the Past 205 Million Years and the Evolution of Large Placental Mammals." *Science* 309 (2005): 2202–4.

Fleming, Ian A., and Mart R. Gross. "Breeding Success of Hatchery and Wild Coho Salmon (*Oncorhynchus kisutch*) in Competition." *Ecological Applications* 3 (1993): 230–45.

Fleming, Ian A., and Erik Petersson. "The Ability of Released, Hatchery Salmonids to Breed and Contribute to the Natural Productivity of Wild Populations." *Nordic Journal of Freshwater Research* 75 (2001): 71–98.

Flora of North America Editorial Committee, eds. *Flora of North America North of Mexico*. Vol. 4. New York and Oxford: http://www.eFloras.org, 1993+.

Flores, Dan. "Bison Ecology and Bison Diplomacy: The Southern Plains from 1800 to 1850." *Journal of American History* 78 (1991): 465–85.

Fox-Dobbs, Kena, Thomas A. Stidham, Gabriel J. Bowen, Steven D. Emslie, and Paul L. Koch. "Dietary Controls on Extinction versus Survival among Avian Megafauna in the Late Pleistocene." *Geology* 34 (2006): 685–88.

Franklin, Jerry F., Fredrick J. Swanson, Mark E. Harmon, David A. Perry, Thomas A. Spies, Virginia H. Dale, Arthur McKee, et al. "Effects of Global Climate Change on Forests in Northwestern North America." *Northwest Environmental Journal* 7 (1991): 233–54.

Gealy, David R., S. Gurusiddaiah, and Alex G. Ogg Jr. "Isolation and Characterization of Metabolites from *Pseudomonas syringae*–Strain 3366 and Their Phytotoxicity against Certain Weed and Crop Species." *Weed Science* 44 (1996): 383–92.

Gibson, James R. *Farming the Frontier: The Agricultural Opening of the Oregon Country, 1786 to 1846.* Seattle: University of Washington Press, 1985.

Harlan, Richard. "On a New Fossil Genus of the Order Enalio Sauir (of Conybeare)." *Journal of the Academy of Natural Sciences of Philadelphia* 3 (1824): 331–37.

Hickman, James C. *The Jepson Manual: Higher Plants of California.* Berkeley and Los Angeles: University of California Press, 1993.

Hofreiter, M., H. N. Poinar, W. G. Spaulding, K. Bauer, P. S. Martin, G. Possnert, and S. Pääbo. "A Molecular Analysis of Ground Sloth Diet through the Last Glaciation." *Molecular Ecology* 9 (2000): 1975–84.

Hu, Wen-Jing, Scott A. Harding, Jrhau Lung, Jacqueline L. Popko, John Ralph, Douglas D. Stokke, Chung-Jui Tsai, and Vincent L. Chiang. "Repression of Lignin Biosynthesis Promotes Cellulose Accumulation and Growth in Transgenic Trees." *Nature Biotechnology* 17 (1999): 808–12.

Jackson, Donald. *Letters of the Lewis and Clark Expedition with Related Documents, 1783–1854.* 2d ed. Vol. 1. Urbana: University of Illinois Press, 1978.

Janzen, Daniel H., and Paul S. Martin. "Neotropical Anachronisms: The Fruits the Gomphotheres Ate." *Science* 215 (1982): 19–27.

Jefferson, Thomas. "A Memoir of the Discovery of Certain Bones of a Quadruped of the Clawed Type in the Western Parts of Virginia." *Transactions of the American Philosophical Society* 4 (1799): 246–60.

Jones, Kevin T., and David B. Madsen. "Further Experiments in Native Food Procurement." *Utah Archaeology* 4 (1991): 68–76.

Karban, Richard, Mikaela Huntzinger, and A. C. McCall. "The Specificity of Eavesdropping on Sagebrush by Other Plants." *Ecology* 85 (2004): 1846–52.

Kendall, Katherine C., and Stephen F. Arno. "Whitebark Pine: An Important but Endangered Wildlife Resource." In *Proceedings— Symposium on Whitebark Pine Ecosystems: Ecology and Management of a High-Mountain Resource,* ed. W. C. Schmidt and K. J. McDonald, 264–73. USDA Forest Service General Technical Report INT-270. Bozeman, Mont.: USDA Forest Service, 1990.

Knapp, Paul A. "Window of Opportunity: The Climatic Conditions of the Lewis and Clark Expedition of 1804–1806." *Bulletin of the American Meteorological Society* 85 (2004): 1289–303.

Koch, George W., Stephen C. Sillett, Gregory M. Jennings, and Stephen D. Davis. "The Limits to Tree Height." *Nature* 428 (2004): 851–54.

Krenzelok, E. P., and F. J. Provost. "The 10 Most Common Plant Exposures Reported to Poison Information Centers in the United States." *Journal of Natural Toxins* 4 (1995): 195–202.

Lackey, Robert T. "Restoring Wild Salmon to the Pacific Northwest: Chasing an Illusion?" In *What We Don't Know about Pacific Northwest Fish Runs: An Inquiry into Decision-Making,* ed. Patricia Koss and Mike Katz, 91–143. Portland: Portland State University Press, 2000.

Laliberte, Andrea S., and William J. Ripple. "Range Contractions of North American Carnivores and Ungulates." *BioScience* 54 (2004): 123–38.

Lang, Ronald F., Robert D. Richard, Paul E. Parker, and Lloyd Wendel. "Release and Establishment of Diffuse and Spotted

Knapweed Biocontrol Agents by USDA, APHIS, PPQ, in the United States." *Pan-Pacific Entomologist* 76 (2000): 197–218.

Lanner, Ronald M. *Made for Each Other: A Symbiosis of Birds and Pines.* New York: Oxford University Press, 1996.

Leonard, Jennifer A., Robert K. Wayne, and Alan Cooper. "Population Genetics of Ice Age Brown Bears." *Proceedings of the National Academy of Sciences of the United States of America* 97 (2000): 1651–54.

Leopold, Aldo. *A Sand County Almanac.* New York: Oxford University Press, 1966.

Lichatowich, James A. *Salmon without Rivers.* Washington, D.C.: Island Press, 1999.

Lipscomb, Albert A., and Albert E. Bergh. *The Writings of Thomas Jefferson.* Memorial Edition. 20 vols. Washington, D.C.: Thomas Jefferson Memorial Association, 1903–1904.

Mack, R. N. "Invasion of *Bromus tectorum L.* into Western North America: An Ecological Chronicle." *Agro-ecosystems* 7 (1981): 145–65.

Mackenzie, Alexander. *Journal of the Voyage to the Pacific.* Ed. W. Sheppe. New York: Dover Publications, 1995. Originally published as *Voyages from Montreal* (1801).

Mancilla-Margalli, N. A., and M. G. López. "Generation of Maillard Compounds from Inulin during the Thermal Processing of *Agave tequiana* Weber var. *azul.*" *Journal of Agricultural and Food Chemistry* 50 (2002): 806–12.

Marshall, Alan G. "Nez Perce Social Groups: An Ecological Interpretation." Ph.D. diss., Washington State University, 1977.

Martin, Paul S. "The Discovery of America." *Science* 179 (1973): 969–74.

Martin, Paul S., and Christine R. Szuter. "War Zones and Game Sinks in Lewis and Clark's West." *Conservation Biology* 13 (1999): 36–45.

Mattson, David J., R. Gerald Wright, Katherine C. Kendall, and Clifford J. Martinka. "Grizzly Bears." U.S. Department of the Interior, National Biological Service. http://biology.usgs.gov/s+t/noframe/c032.htm.

McCourt, Richard M., and Earle E. Spamer. "The Botanical Legacy of Lewis and Clark: The Most Famous Collection You Never Heard Of." *Plant Science Bulletin* 49 (2003): 126–30.

McDonald, Jerry N. *North American Bison: Their Classification and Evolution.* Berkeley and Los Angeles: University of California Press, 1981.

Mote, P., D. Canning, D. Fluharty, R. Francis, J. Franklin, A. Hamlet, M. Hershman, et al. "Impacts of Climate Variability and Change in the Pacific Northwest." The JISAO Climate Impacts Group, University of Washington, 2004. http://www.cses.washington.edu/cig.

Moulton, Gary. *The Journals of the Lewis and Clark Expedition.* Vols. 1–13. Lincoln: University of Nebraska Press, 1983–2001. Also available online at the University of Nebraska Press, University of Nebraska–Lincoln Libraries–Electronic Text Center, http://lewisandclarkjournals.unl.edu.

Muir, John. *Our National Parks.* Boston: Houghton Mifflin, 1901.

Mullin, M. P., S. Peacock, D. C. Loewen, and N. J. Turner. "Macronutrients Content of Yellow Glacier Lily and Balsamroot Vegetables Used by Indigenous Peoples of Northwestern North America." *Food Research International* 30 (1997): 769–75.

Murray, Michael P., and Mary Rasmussen. "Status of Whitebark Pine in Crater Lake National Park." 2000. http://oregonstate.edu/ornhic/publications.html.

Nash, Roderick. *Wilderness and the American Mind.* New Haven: Yale University Press, 1982.

National Fire and Aviation Executive Board Policy Directives Task

Group. "Wildland Fire Use Implementation Procedures Reference Guide." http://www.nifc.gov/fire_policy/index.htm.

National Wilderness Institute. "State by State Government Land Ownership." http://www.nwi.org/Maps/LandChart.html.

Oak Ridge National Laboratory. "Popular Poplars." http://bioenergy.ornl.gov/misc/poplars.html.

Olson, Bret E., and Rick G. Kelsey. "Effect of *Centaurea maculosa* on Sheep Rumen Microbial Activity and Mass in Vitro." *Journal of Chemical Ecology* 23 (1997): 1131–44.

Oregon Department of Agriculture. "Economic Analysis of Containment Programs, Damages, and Production Losses from Noxious Weeds in Oregon." 2000. http://egov.oregon.gov/ODA/PLANT/docs/pdf/weed_body_a.pdf.

Ownbey, Marion. "A Monograph of the Genus *Calochortus*." *Annals of the Missouri Botanical Garden* 27 (1940): 371–560.

Pacific States Marine Fisheries Commission. "Northern Pikeminnow Sport Reward Fishery." http://www.pikeminnow.org.

Paine, R. T. "Intertidal Community Structure: Experimental Studies on the Relationship between a Dominant Competitor and Its Principal Predator." *Oecologia* 15 (1974): 93–120.

Patterson, Thomas B., and Thomas J. Givnish. "Geographic Cohesion, Chromosomal Evolution, Parallel Adaptive Radiations, and Consequent Floral Adaptations in *Calochortus* (Calochortaceae): Evidence from a cpDNA Phylogeny." *New Phytologist* 161 (2003): 253–64.

Pearson, Dean E., and Ragan M. Callaway. "Biological Control Agents Elevate Hantavirus by Subsidizing Deer Mouse Populations." *Ecology Letters* 9 (2006): 443–50.

Pearson, Paul N., and Martin R. Palmer. "Atmospheric Carbon Dioxide Concentrations over the Past 60 Million Years." *Nature* 406 (2000): 695–99.

Pfosser, Martin, and Franz Speta. "Phylogenetics of Hyacinthaceae Based on Plastid DNA Sequences." *Annals of the Missouri Botanical Garden* 86 (1999): 852–75.

Pimentel, David, Lori Lach, Rodolfo Zuniga, and Doug Morrison. "Environmental and Economic Costs Associated with Non-indigenous Species in the United States." *BioScience* 50 (1999): 53–65.

Poinar, H. N., C. Schwars, J. Qi, B. Shapiro, R. D. E. MacPhee, B. Buigues, A. Tikhonov, et al. "Metagenomics to Paleogenomics: Large-Scale Sequencing of Mammoth DNA." *Science* 311 (2006): 392–94.

Preston, Richard. "Tall for Its Age." *New Yorker,* October 9, 2006, 32–36.

Reveal, James L. "Making Drawings and Writing Descriptions," Discovering Lewis & Clark. http://www.lewis-clark.org.

Reveal, James L., Gary E. Moulton, and Alfred E. Schuyler. "The Lewis and Clark Collections of Vascular Plants." *Proceedings of the Academy of Natural Sciences of Philadelphia* 149 (1999): 1–64.

Rhodes, Richard. *The Ozarks.* New York: Time-Life Books, 1974.

Ripple, William J., and Robert L. Beschta. "Wolf Reintroduction, Predation Risk, and Cottonwood Recovery in Yellowstone National Park." *Forest Ecology and Management* 184 (2003): 299–313.

Robbins, Jim. "Lessons from the Wolf." *Scientific American* (June 2004): 76–81.

Roosevelt, Theodore. *Ranch Life and the Hunting-Trail.* New York: Century, 1888.

Schambach, Frank F. "Osage Orange Bows, Indian Horses, and the Blackland Prairie of Northeastern Texas." In *Blackland Prairies of the Gulf Coastal Plain: Nature, Culture, and Sustainability,* ed. Evan Peacock and Timothy Schauwecker, 212–36. Tuscaloosa: University of Alabama Press, 2003.

Schroeder, Michael A., David W. Hays, Michael F. Livingston, Leray E. Stream, John E. Jacobson, and D. John Pierce. "Changes in the Distribution and Abundance of Sage Grouse in Washington." *Northwestern Naturalist* 81 (2000): 104–12.

Southerton, Simon G. *Losing a Lost Tribe: Native Americans, DNA, and the Mormon Church.* Salt Lake City: Signature Books, 2004.

Thwaites, Reuben. *Original Journals of the Lewis and Clark Expedition.* 7 vols. Newark: Dodd, Mead, 1904.

Tocqueville, Alexis de. *Democracy in America.* Edited by Phillips Bradley. New York: Vintage Books, 1945.

Union of Concerned Scientists. "Climate Change in the Hawkeye State." http://www.ucsusa.org/global_environment/global_warming/page.cfm?pageID=1306.

U.S. Department of the Interior, National Park Service. "Wolves of Yellowstone." http://www.nps.gov/yell/naturescience/wolves.htm.

U.S. Department of the Interior, U.S. Fish and Wildlife Service. "Rocky Mountain Wolf Recovery 2006 Annual Report." http://www.fws.gov/mountain-prairie/species/mammals/wolf/annualrpt06/index.htm.

U.S. Department of the Interior, U.S. Geological Survey. "Digital Representation of 'Atlas of United States Trees' by Elbert L. Little, Jr." http://www.esp.cr.usgs.gov/info/veg-clim/.

van Frankenhuyzen, Kees, and Tannis Beardmore. "Current Status and Environmental Impact of Transgenic Forest Trees." *Canadian Journal of Forest Research* 34 (2004): 1163–80.

van Pelt, Robert. *Forest Giants of the Pacific Coast.* Seattle: University of Washington Press, 2001.

Vehrencamp, Sandra L., Jack W. Bradbury, and Robert M. Gibson. "The Energetic Cost of Display in Male Sage Grouse." *Animal Behaviour* 38 (1989): 885–96.

Wang, X., and G. R. Gibson. "Effects of the In-vitro Fermentation of Oligofructose and Inulin by Bacteria Growing in the Human Large Intestine." *Journal of Applied Bacteriology* 75 (1993): 373–80.

Waring, Richard H., and Jerry F. Franklin. "Evergreen Coniferous Forests of the Pacific Northwest." *Science* 204 (1979): 1380–86.

Weidensaul, Scott. "Sage Grouse Strut Their Stuff." *Smithsonian Magazine,* June 2001.

Wetzel, S. C., C. Demmers, and J. S. Greenwood. "Seasonally Fluctuating Bark Proteins Are a Potential Form of Nitrogen Storage in 3 Temperate Hardwoods." *Planta* 178 (1989): 275–81.

Wildland Fire Leadership Council. "Large Fire Suppression Costs: Strategies for Cost Management." 2004. http://www.iafc.org/grants/wildland_fire.asp.

Wiley, R. Haven. "Territoriality and Non-random Mating in Sage Grouse (*Centrocercus urophasianus*)." *Animal Behavior Monographs* 6 (1973): 85–169.

Wilkinson, T. "Rediscovering Lewis and Clark's America." *Nature Conservancy* 54 (2004): 34–41.

Willamette Valley Livability Forum. "Oregon's Willamette Valley: Facts and Figures." http://www.lcog.org/wvlf/info.html.

Wistar, Caspar. "An Account of Two Heads Found in the Morass, Called Big Lick, and Presented to the Society, by Mr. Jefferson." *Transactions of the Philosophical Society,* n.s., 1 (1818): 375–80.

Young, James A., and Charlie D. Clements. Purshia: *The Wild and Bitter Roses.* Reno: University of Nevada Press, 2002.

Zwickel, Fred C., and Michael A. Schroeder. "Grouse of the Lewis and Clark Expedition, 1803 to 1806." *Northwestern Naturalist* 84 (2003): 1–19.

INDEX